D1286873

Year 'Round Walleyes

Fishing The Four Seasons

Year 'Round Walleyes

Fishing The Four Seasons

By

Mark Martin

Year 'Round Walleyes
Fishing The Four Seasons

Brief quotations may be used in critical articles and reviews. For any other reproduction of this book, illustrations and photographs, including electronic, mechanical, photocopying, recording, or other means, written permission must be given by the publisher.

Copyright © 1998 by Mark Martin
First printing 1998
Printed in the United States of America

Cover photo by Mark Romanack
Cover design by RuthAnn Lueck
Layout and design by Kay Richey
Electronically created camera-ready copy by
  KLR Communications, Inc.
  POB 192
  Grawn, MI 49637

Art illustrations courtesy of In-Fisherman & Gene Moore

Year 'Round Walleyes, Fishing The Four Seasons / by Mark Martin
Walleyes / History / Fishing / Michigan - North America

ISBN 0-9659291-0-8 Softcover

Acknowledgments

A book of this size isn't the work of just one person. Many people have offered a helping hand at one time or another.

Some helped by nudging me in the right direction. Others offered ideas, some proof read the copy, some provided timely editing, and others were there to offer moral support when it was needed the most.

A big "thank you" goes to Dave and Kay Richey. Without their editing and layout skills, this book would never have been possible. They coaxed, cajoled and, when necessary, whipped me into shape. Their book production skills rival that of any eastern big-name publishing house, and they rode herd on me and my book from beginning to end.

Book writing and editing and final layout is a skill that only comes with years of experience. For a tournament walleye fishermen, attempting a book of this scope was a daunting project. My countless friends stuck by me, and you now hold the results in your hands.

My sponsors contributed greatly to my success, both on and off the water, and before and after book publication. Without their paid advertisements, the reader would have been shortchanged by a lack of indepth drawings and photos. Because of their help, the finished book is crammed with information, detailed photos and many illustrations.

A debt of gratitude also goes to my Dad and Mom and my grandparents. If Dad and my grandfather hadn't taken me fishing at an early age, and planted the seed to become a walleye fisherman, this book would have been nothing more than a dream. Their efforts and love at an early age opened my eyes to a big and wonderful world of fishing. They allowed me to fish as a youngster on Michigan's Lloyd's Bayou and Spring Lake, and later on

Muskegon Lake. Those early family adventures enabled me to develop a love for a variety of gamefish, and I'm deeply indebted to my family.

Friends who have fished with me for years were helpful during this learning process. Media friends are thanked because they wrote up my many experiences, covered my successes, and helped establish my career. Reporters from radio, television, newspapers and magazines promoted my accomplishments because they knew I like to teach people how to fish. Twenty years ago, Mark Martin was just a young man that liked to fish, but now, with the media's help, I've been able to help others enjoy the sport I love and catch more walleyes in the process.

One man — Gary Roach — is owed a warm and special thanks. This man, universally known as Mr. Walleye, took time to help channel and refocus my abilities. He pointed out subtle differences in my fishing techniques that have taken me to a new and higher level of expertise.

Roach also helped by donating his decades of walleye knowledge. The result is that I'm now light years ahead of where I would be if he hadn't helped during my early tournament years. Thanks Gary!

I've saved the best for last. My wife Paula, and daughter Rachael, have accompanied me on many fishing trips. They've offered words of encouragement during tournaments, have never complained when I've had to leave home for days, weeks or a month, because they know that walleye fishing is my life. I know it's been hard for them but Paula keeps everything on track. Her help has enabled me to become a success in the walleye industry. Thanks Honey!

In the event that I've missed somebody, be they friends or sponsors, be assured it wasn't intentional. There just wasn't enough room for another chapter in this book, and that's how much room it would take to include everyone by name.

For one and all, a heartfelt and sincere thank you.

Dedication

This book is dedicated to my wife Paula. Without her help and encouragement my life as a professional fisherman wouldn't be possible.

Preface

The first time I met Mark Martin I was doing a seminar at the BASSARAMA in Michigan. He came over and introduced himself, and we've been friends ever since.

Mark is a very good fisherman, who pays attention to what's happening around him at all times.

We have fished as a team and share information at all tournaments.

He won the first PWT championship, and finished in the top ten in 1997, which is quite a feat.

Mark will stop and help all fisher people with any information he has that will help them catch more fish.

I would encourage anyone who wants to become a better fisherman to buy this book. It is loaded with tons of information and graphics. You will want to read it over and over.

Good luck and good fishin',

Gary Roach

Table of Contents

Walleye History

Walleyes have been around for countless centuries, and down through time, they have become an expensive and important food fish for commercial and sport fishermen. Their original range encompassed much of the Midwestern states and eastern and central Canadian provinces, and its range has grown over the last century.

Good to excellent walleye populations exist from Canada's Northwest Territories' Great Slave Lake south and east through Alberta, Saskatchewan and Manitoba. They are found in the Dakotas, Minnesota, Montana, Wyoming, Wisconsin, Michigan, south into Kentucky and Tennessee, and east through the St. Lawrence River drainage system and north into Labrador.

Fish plantings have stocked walleyes in waters where they never existed before. Classic examples include the Columbia River, Arizona, Arkansas, Colorado, New Mexico and Texas to name just a few states that have jumped onto the walleye bandwagon.

Add most of the Great Lakes as other major walleye producers. Of the five huge inland seas, Lakes Erie, Huron and Ontario have first-rate walleye fisheries.

Some great walleye fishing for jumbo fish is found in Lake Michigan's Little and Big Bay de Nocs, and Green Bay, and these major bays are magnets for walleyes. Lake Superior, even with its extremely cold water, produces some good walleye fishing in Minnesota's Duluth Harbor and St. Louis River; in nearby Ashland Bay at Ashland, Wisconsin, and in Michigan's Waiska Bay and Izaak Walton (Mosquito) Bay near Brimley. Lake St. Clair, on the doorstep of Detroit, offers a bonanza of walleye fishing activity near millions of people.

Photo by Gary Roach

Department of Natural Resources shocking boat returning from a successful trip collecting walleye's for the egg taking program for restocking lakes, rivers and reservoirs.

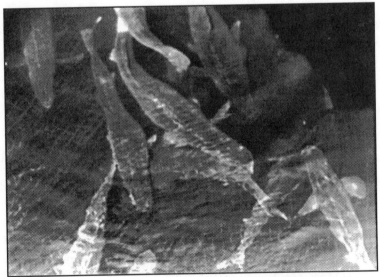

Photo by Ron Hunter, Judd's Resort

The DNR uses a net to trap and take spawn from spring walleyes.

Major river systems like the Columbia, Colorado, Illinois, Mississippi, Missouri, Ohio, Susquehanna and Tennessee have excellent numbers of fish. Many major tributaries of those rivers also produce good numbers of fish for local and visiting anglers.

The walleye is a fish of many nicknames: Dore (Quebec), 'eye, glass-eye, hornfish, jack, jack salmon, marble-eye, pickerel, pike-perch, wall-eyed pike, white salmon, yellow pike, yellow pickerel and yellow pike-perch.

As a gamefish, walleyes are considered the No. 1 sportfish by many anglers. They grow to large size, and although the world-record fish weighed about 25 pounds, there are questions concerning its authentic weight.

Nonetheless, walleyes of 10 pounds — while never common anywhere — are caught in many locations across North America with some regularity. It takes a fish of 15 pounds to raise eyebrows or create a sensation.

These gamefish were heavily fished by commercial netters for many years and in many areas until enlightened federal, provincial and state authorities determined they were more valuable as a sport fish than as a commercial species. The commercial catch from Lake Erie between 1940-1944 averaged almost 3.7 million pounds annually, and that amounts to a pile of fillets.

Sexual maturity among walleyes is the trigger for the spring spawn. Spawning can take place any time from March through May (earlier in southern states and later in northern states and Canada), and the major contributing factor are weather conditions and proper water temperature. Some spawning will take place once the water temperatures approach 40 degrees F., but more activity is noted as water temperatures reach 44-50 degrees.

Many fish spawn in rivers over a bottom of gravel, rock and rubble. Lake spawning takes place on shoals as shallow as one foot to depths of several feet, and it's thought that larger fish (the females are always the largest) will spawn in slightly deeper water over gravel and rock.

Spawning can take place during day or night, but most of the

action happens after dark. It's not uncommon for several males to accompany a large female. Tests conducted 50 years ago on Michigan's Lake Gogebic in the Upper Peninsula showed a high male-to-female ratio. Of the 7,226 adult and subadult walleyes captured, examined and tagged, 4,315 adult fish were checked. Eighty-nine percent (3,841) were males. As the spawning season progressed, the male-to-female ratio went down. An interesting thing about that study was that most of the spawn was completed within one week.

One of North America's finest walleye streams is the Detroit River. This large river separates Michigan from Ontario, and it receives a huge run of walleyes. Studies indicate that walleyes from Lake Huron, Lake St. Clair and Lake Erie make up the spawning run, and many of the lake fish use this fast flowing river as a spawning site. Other nearby streams like Ontario's Thames River receive good

numbers of big spawning walleyes as well, and parts of Michigan's Clinton River and St. Clair River systems also get a spawning run.

Most of this spawn occurs over two to three weeks, depending on water temperature and prevailing weather conditions. The spring spawn is largely influenced by the natural funneling of water from Lake Huron. This huge body of water funnels down into the St. Clair River at Port Huron, Michigan and Sarnia, Ontario, and then empties into Lake St. Clair. The water flows through Lake St. Clair into the Detroit River before draining into Lake Erie.

Lake Huron warms slowly, and ice is slow to leave the lake. As a rule, the walleye spawn doesn't really kick off until after ice-out in Lake Huron. Floating ice breaks up even more as it passes through the St. Clair River and through Lake St. Clair.

In most years, the spawn kicks off in mid- to late-April, but the spring of 1997 featured a slow breakup of lake ice, and some of the best fishing for big spawning females didn't take place until the first week of May.

Walleye fry hatch in May or June, depending on location and water temperature, and the tiny fry live in shallow water for several weeks before gradually progressing out into the open lake where they live a pelagic existence before heading into deep water in September and October. Their diet consists of insects (often mayfly nymphs and adults) and small fish (often perch and suckers). As these walleye fry and young-of-the-year fish mature, tiny forage fish represent their dominant food source.

Crayfish and insects are common food sources, and in some Midwest areas where lakes freeze during winter months, midge larvae and leeches are consumed.

Two close cousins to the walleye are the sauger and saugeye. Sauger often are smaller than walleyes, but there are many other differences. Sauger can tolerate warmer, dirtier and more turgid water and they often live in deeper water than walleyes.

Body coloration and fin markings are other items for easy fish identification. A sauger has rows of dark spots on the first dorsal fin, whereas walleyes have a larger black blotch at the base of the dorsal fin.

Instead of the smaller spots, the sauger lacks the white tip on the lower lobe of its tail while this white tail-tip is a characteristic of walleyes. Sauger are rather brassy colored along the sides, and they have a dark brownish-black irregularly patterned blotches along the lateral line. These blotches extend above and below the lateral line, and are entirely absent on walleyes.

Both sauger and walleye have large canine-type teeth and the milky or glassy looking eye. Few sauger live in Michigan waters

Photo by Randy Bandstra

A 2-lb. sauger caught on a Northland Bottom Bouncer and spinner.Note the dark blotches along the lateral lines, and spots on dorsal fin.

anymore but they are quite common in the Dakotas, Illinois, Indiana, Montana, Ohio, Pennsylvania, Wisconsin and Wyoming.

Saugeye are hybrid crosses between a sauger and a walleye, and like most hybrids, they are infertile. Cross-breeding occurs naturally where both species are found in the same waters, and hatcheries often cross-breed the two gamefish to produce the faster growing saugeye.

The saugeye has a milky eye like a saugers or walleye, but there is no white tip on the bottom lobe of the tail. Body coloration is similar to that of a walleye, and the only way I can tell a saugeye from a walleye is the missing white tail-tip.

 **19**

Photo by Dave Dulaney
This saugeye was caught using a Northland Fireball jig and minnow.

Walleyes are nomads. Some walleyes have traveled as much as 200 miles although such migratory movements in lake or river are usually much less.

This could perhaps explain why anglers who catch large numbers of walleyes one day, and return the next only to find the area barren of fish. I've often seen nightly movements like this on Muskegon Lake while guiding fishermen.

My clients and I will hook fish in one area after hearing them feed on or near the surface. The feeding frenzy may last only a few minutes before the surface noise ends. Five minutes later we may encounter a similar feeding spree several hundred yards farther up or down the lake. In most cases, this movement is triggered by moving

Dave Dulaney caught this walleye on Saginaw Bay in Michigan.

forage fish.

As alewives, gizzard shad or other forage fish move, we find that the walleyes will move with them. Walleyes, like many predatory gamefish, are driven by the movements of their prey.

Walleyes are school fish, and schools can be small or large. These schools hold more fish when they are young, but as walleyes get older, the number of fish in a school goes down.

One thing that seems to hold true regardless of where walleyes are caught is they tend to school with other fish of similar size. Catch one three-pounder from a school, and chances are that other fish in that group will weigh about the same. Obviously, because of size and longevity, schools of trophy 10-pounders are rare. If you know

 **21**

of a nearby school of big fish like this, give me a call.

It's long been said that walleyes are gamefish that favor low-light levels. Much of their spawning is done at night, and much of their feeding is nocturnal — especially in clear-water lakes. Fish found in dark or stained water can and will feed during daylight hours, and the same often applies to clear-water lakes under heavy cloud cover.

If anything should stick in the mind of readers, it 's this: Fish the low light level periods of dusk and dawn; fish on overcast days; fish deep water on clear lakes, fish near structure that breaks up direct sunlight into the depths; fish mudlines or dirty water whenever possible, and fish where walleyes are found.

Light levels on lakes can change, and in many areas, zebra mussel infestations have changed the habits of walleyes. Zebra mussels filter food particles and zooplankton from the water, and in the process, cleanse the water. Lakes Erie and St. Clair, both in the shadow of Detroit's skyscrapers, are much cleaner today than 10 years ago.

Cleaner water is good ... up to a point. But clean water allows greater light penetration, and that can be bad. Fifteen years ago, Lake Erie boat fishermen considered good visibility in water to be six inches. Today, many parts of Lake Erie are clean enough to see objects in six to 10 feet of water.

The problem with greater light penetration is that it stimulates

Photo by Tom Newstrom

Best fishing comes at twilight, either dawn or dusk.

weed growth. Whenever I give a slide presentation in the Detroit area, anglers come to chat and complain about the lack of walleyes in nearby Lake St. Clair.

This lake, equidistant between Lake Huron and Lake Erie, is shallow. It also was the first lake in the United States to be infected with zebra mussels. These mollusks arrived from European countries in the bilge water of ocean-going freighters. The ships discharged bilge water in Lake St. Clair, and the little rascals multiplied faster than rabbits. Now, nine years later, zebra mussels are everywhere.

This infestation, and the resulting filtration of Lake St. Clair water, stimulated weed growth. The lake has many times more weeds today than five years ago.

Complaints of fewer walleyes fall on deaf ears. The fish are there; the problem is anglers have not learned to fish the weeds to catch them.

Of course, pointing that out to anglers is like a slapping them in the face. They prefer to believe the problem lies in fewer gamefish rather than their inability or lack of success at catching weedy walleyes. Explaining that is a no-win situation.

Walleye fishing has become big business. Bass anglers often claim their gamefish as the No. 1 sportsfish in North America. That may or may not be true, and I'm not out to argue the point with anyone.

All I know is that walleyes and walleye fishing has exploded over the last 10 years. In Michigan where I live, salmon had a leglock on angler attention for 20 years, but in the late 1980s, disease and other factors caused this long love affair with salmon to sour.

The sport of catching walleyes stepped in to fill the void left by salmon. Think about it: the walleye limit was five fish per angler, except in Lake Erie where it was 10, and people could head out on the lake in a tin boat or cabin cruiser, and catch a limit in short order.

As walleye research and plantings grew, the gamefish took hold of state anglers and hasn't let go. The same phenomenon has occurred in countless other regions through the east, Midwest and southern states. Anglers flock to Canada for a near-wilderness walleye

experience. They are fun to catch and taste great at dinner.

With this explosion in interest has come tremendous advances in fishing tackle. Tournament anglers like me have helped lead the way. We've helped devise new lures, new rods and reels, new lines and countless new techniques that help anglers perfect their fishing presentations and up their catch.

We've seen new magazines that are vertically slanted to walleyes, and we've seen television shows and videos by the dozens as they expound at length on how to catch walleyes. All of this is good for the casual or more advanced angler.

More and more detailed data is released each year about walleyes and how to catch them. Tackle companies no longer produce make-do equipment; those companies that produce tackle for walleye fisherman are producing quality merchandise at an affordable price.

Anglers now have a wide choice of equipment to use. New lures from crankbaits, crawler harnesses, jigs and spoons have come on the market in recent years. Boat companies like Lund are producing craft designed by and for the walleye fisherman. The same is true of other equipment manufactured by anglers for anglers.

Walleye fishing has come of age. Anglers are more informed than ever before, and that is as it should be.

With that thought in mind, let's move right in to the next chapter. Curl up in an easy chair, kick back and study this book. It will make you a better walleye fisherman.

I guarantee it.

(L) Paula and Mark Martin enjoying a Canadian shore lunch. The fish was woven on willow branches and cooked over a open fire.

Photo by Floyd Olsen

The Well-Equipped Walleye Boat

A carpenter takes on a job with a well equipped assortment of hammers, saws and other necessary tools; a mechanic approaches his work with socket wrenches and other needed equipment, so it only stands to reason that a walleye fisherman should consider owning the proper tools for his trade.

Rods, reels, lines and lures are important, but more critical in my mind is owning a well equipped boat. A boat with the proper equipment makes walleye fishing easier and more productive because the angler has had enough foresight to prepare himself for any boating or fishing eventuality.

We've all seen anglers with a 12-foot aluminum boat. Two rods and a flasher unit make up the person's equipment. Chances are he will catch some fish, but when a storm arises or a specific fishing situation pops up suddenly, the angler isn't prepared to deal with adverse fishing circumstances.

Choosing a boat, motor, trailer, flasher, graph and other walleye fishing equipment is as personal a choice as the color of your morning toothbrush. However, with that being said, today's modern walleye angler should be prepared to spend enough money on his/her equipment to make the fishing experience as safe and fun filled as possible.

This sport, like any other, requires a sizable investment in hard earned dollars. The day of outfitting a fishing boat for two thousand dollars is a thing of the past. A well equipped walleye boat and tow vehicle, one that can handle almost any situation Mother Nature can throw at you, means spending a healthy chunk of money.

A well equipped walleye boat and tow vehicle.

To put everything in perspective, an auto mechanic won't be able to do his job well with only socket wrenches and a screwdriver. A carpenter with only a hand saw and a hammer will find few jobs.

The walleye fisherman with only the bare necessities will catch a few fish but limit catches under all types of weather conditions are an impossibility without the proper tools. I know from sad experience: in my earlier days before hitting the tournament trail, I tried to make do with the minimum amount of boating and fishing equipment.

It didn't take long to realize that certain equipment — a well made boat, the proper outboard and kicker motors, electric trolling motors, and a wise choice of fishing rods and reels and lures — would make fishing easier, more fun and more exciting.

I studied the boat and motor market at great length before deciding what I needed to fish walleyes under all but the foulest weather conditions. Let's face it: an angler who is scared of three-foot waves will spend most of their time on the beach dreaming about fishing rather than going out and doing it.

My first choice for a walleye boat is a deep-V aluminum hull that is riveted together for maximum sturdiness. This type of hull cleaves through waves, provides a comfortable ride, and is built for strength and safety on the water.

An aluminum hull can withstand being bumped on shoreline rocks, cut by skim ice early and late in the year, being banged against docks, and capable of absorbing heavy waves whenever necessary. I never advocate taking chances on the water, but if a walleye fisherman fishes enough, sooner or later they will be caught far from port in a storm. This is when every dollar spent on a good boat will pay for itself. A strong hull and reliable outboard provides anglers with the knowledge that with proper handling, the boat will carry them safely home.

My Lund Pro V is built with plenty of room. It has a deep hull, wide beam and plenty of rod and tackle storage areas. My boat comes with an extra large battery compartment for the 36-volt system.

There is a livewell and a baitwell in both bow and stern, and aerator systems pump in fresh water while running to keep bait and fish frisky. Laws mandate built-in flotation in the hull, bow and stern, and this provides for a more comfortable ride and enables the craft to stay afloat even in the worst storm. Rugged I-beam construction makes my fishing boat sturdy and safe in the nastiest of weather conditions.

Roominess is an important factor in a well made fishing boat. Compromise on price and size, and people begin stepping on rods or fighting to maintain their position in rough water. My tournament boat is big enough to throw a party in, and tackle compartments keep unused equipment in a safe place and not underfoot. Roominess should never be compromised, and a big, wide, deep hull with a level floor provides enough room in which to move while providing stable footing.

The walleye fisherman's choice of an outboard motor(s) is an important consideration. My outboards are Mariners, and the big 225-horsepower motor is peppy enough to get the boat up on plane quickly, and can move me one mile or 20 miles fast enough that I miss very little prime fishing time. One critical point to remember: each boat has a listed recommendation for engine size, horsepower and load carrying capacity. Buy a motor that is the maximum recommended size for your boat.

The Well Equipped Boat

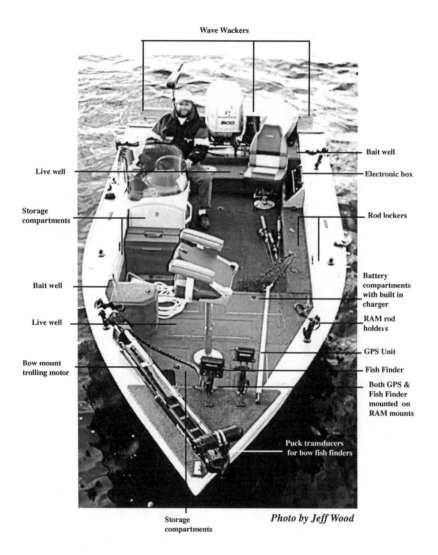

Wave Wackers

Bait well

Live well

Electronic box

Storage compartments

Rod lockers

Bait well

Battery compartments with built in charger

Live well

RAM rod holders

GPS Unit

Bow mount trolling motor

Fish Finder

Both GPS & Fish Finder mounted on RAM mounts

Puck transducers for bow fish finders

Storage compartments

Photo by Jeff Wood

The Well Equipped Boat

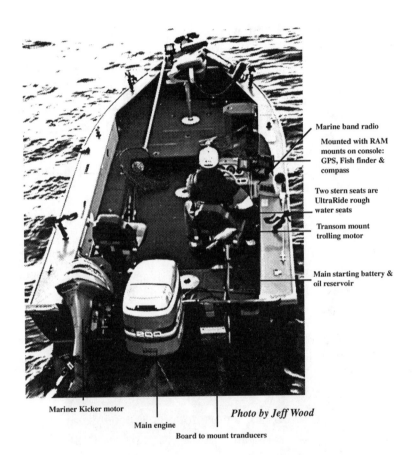

Marine band radio

Mounted with RAM mounts on console: GPS, Fish finder & compass

Two stern seats are UltraRide rough water seats

Transom mount trolling motor

Main starting battery & oil reservoir

Mariner Kicker motor

Main engine

Board to mount tranducers

Photo by Jeff Wood

I also use a transom-mounted 9.9 Mariner kicker motor on the stern. There are many uses for the smaller motor in various trolling applications, and besides handling these fishing jobs, the second motor provides a comfort factor. Knowing there are two outboards on the boat provides an additional sense of safety for anglers.

Kicker motors are made in two cycle and four cycle. A two cycle engine is lighter in weight but requires a gas-oil mixture. A four stroke engine operates on gasoline from the main fuel tank, and they have a separate oil compartment built in for engine lubrication.

Avoid buying an underpowered boat. Many anglers follow this path in the mistaken belief that they can save money which can then be spent on other equipment. A too-small motor reduces power, stability and performance, and will cost an angler more money in the long run.

A maxed-out outboard enables the angler to carry a full load of fishermen, gear and tackle, to get up on plane fast and not have to run at full throttle to stay on plane. Underpowered boats guzzle gas, and in the long run, are more expensive to operate because they must be run harder to stay up on plane, regardless of the load.

Many people wonder why walleye tournament anglers use outboards. Why not an inboard or I/O (inboard/outboard) motor? Outboards are much easier to work on if a problem develops, require less maintenance, and have more reliable performance.

Hydraulic steering is a must for quick maneuverability when following breaklines or dropoffs, and steering with this system is much easier on arms and shoulders during a long day on the water.

The best prop for an outboard motor will provide better performance. A three-blade prop provides the best speed. For total overall performance, a High 5 prop seems to work best in most situations.

This prop responds faster and better on sharp turns, holds the boat on the water surface better, and can climb very tall waves

without blowing out on the top. This means extra safety for the boater-fisherman in rough water. For rough water conditions, anglers need a prop that bites in when ascending a big wave.

Another piece of equipment that I highly recommend is The Edge. It attaches to the top of the lower unit, and is a triangular shaped piece of stainless steel that helps bring the bow down quickly and keeps a boat from cavitating.

Electric start outboards are the best thing since sliced bread. Make sure your batteries are sufficiently charged, and a back-up battery is always good to have along. Trying to start a big outboard by hand is exhausting work, and if it ever happens, your first stop will be to buy a back-up battery.

A manual start kicker motor is easy to use. Just make sure to change plugs often, especially after prolonged trolling, and you'll find the new motors easy to start by hand.

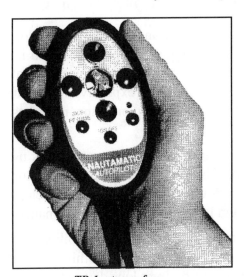

TR-1 sets you free

One unit I've fallen in love with is my TR-1 Autopilot. It attaches to my big motor and operates off a compass and gyro system, and it can be interfaced with my GPS unit. It really comes in handy when trolling a breakline or in open water. It works equally well for forward trolling or back trolling.

Simply point the bow or stern in the direction you wish to troll, and turn it on. It has a cord remote which enables the angler to control both speed and slight course adjustments. I use mine almost every day and wouldn't dream of fishing without it.

Electric trolling motors are a wise investment for any walleye boat. There are two 36-volt MotorGuide 72-pound thrust electric

trolling motors on mine; one is bow mounted and the other is transom mounted, and they enable me to fish almost anywhere. When buying electric trolling motors, purchase long-shaft models. The best shaft length for a walleye boat will be different than those used on bass boats. My preferred shaft length for a bow-mounted electric will be 54-60 inches. A too-short shaft, in rough water, will lift the prop out of the water in wavy conditions and this results in less precise boat control.

The transom height on most walleye boats manufactured these days is 20-25 inches. Choose a transom mounted electric with a shaft long enough so the prop is beneath the boat's hull, and this is especially advantageous when backtrolling.

Choosing the proper batteries for marine electronics is very important. I prefer the oil-filled MotorGuide Thermoil batteries because they hold a charge longer, take a charge faster and require less maintenance. There are no dangerous fumes and no battery terminal corrosion. This makes it a much better system, and these batteries are hooked to a 3-bank built-in charger that requires only an electrical plug-in at the end of a long fishing day.

Wave Wackers are another must, especially for backtrollers, but they are very useful to keep following waves from breaking over the transom while forward trolling or when running with the waves from one area to another.

These accessories are made of molded Plexiglass that are attached to the transom and they fit around the motors. They deflect water away from the stern and engines.

A GPS unit has become a very important tool for today's walleye fisherman, and I wouldn't be without mine. In fact, I have two GPS units; one is mounted in the bow and one of the steering console. My flashers and graph are mounted on the console for easy reading.

I have an Offshore Plastimo compass, imported by Simpson Lawrance, on my boat. It is big enough to read during the day or when lighted at night, and when the compass information is combined with data from my GPS unit, it provides a measure of safety that no walleye fishermen should ignore. This combination allows me to follow a straight and true line, and helps eliminate weaving back and forth while following a plotter trail.

A waterproof marine radio allows contact with other anglers, a quick check of changing weather conditions, and it can save your life.

My mounting system for marine electronics are the best money can buy. I use the Round-A-Mount system because it has a rubber ball mount with arm-type clamps that can be tightened once the unit is in the best position for easy visibility. These units offer a buffer for my electronics, and it helps prevent those hard jolts in rough water that raise havoc with valuable equipment.

Round-A-Mount also manufactures great antenna mounts, rodholders and trolling motor supports. Each one is designed to keep you fishing without a problem.

All-day fishing will take a toll on feet, legs and back. The new custom UltraRide seat suspension has springs, shocks and torsion bars which can be precision set for your weight and for existing wave conditions. Properly positioned and set, this unit will relieve stress and eliminate the pounding that legs and back absorb on a daily basis. A full day on the water, even in rough seas, is a piece of cake with this adjustable seat.

Trailers often are the last thing considered when buying a boat and motor. The opposite should be true although it seldom is with most new boat buyers. They often buy a boat and motor, and then skimp on a trailer.

I'm a strong believer in buying quality. A good trailer will cushion the boat hull and motor while in transit, and good money spent on a fine trailer is a wise investment. My Trailmaster bunk trailer has spare tire, surge brakes and mag wheels with heavy duty radial tires, and my trailer was painted the same color as my Lund boat. It really compliments the whole package.

A bunk-style trailer will cradle the boat without having rollers pounding against the aluminum hull. Surge brakes help with quicker stops, and the radial tires are a must. Bias ply tires build up too much heat on long distance drives during hot summer months, and radials really hold the pavement better.

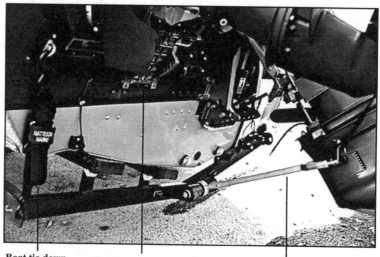

Boat tie down   Kicker motor support   Transom saver for main motor

Good tiedowns are important, and so is a motor support when trailering the boat down the highway because it helps prevent bouncing and possible boat or engine damage on bumpy roads. Mercury makes a handy little support for the kicker motor, and it's money well spent.

A well-equipped walleye boat should meet or exceed U.S. Coast Guard specifications for personal flotation devices (PFDs) and other safety features. Statistics prove that most on-the-water deaths occur by drowning, and it's wise for anglers to have good PFDs aboard for every person. Wearable life jackets are a must, and so too is a throwable ring should someone accidentally fall overboard.

A fire extinguisher is a necessity, and one hopes they will never have to be used. Mine was once used to put out a fire in a house trailer being towed by an elderly couple as they headed for Florida. He didn't have a fire extinguisher, but mine was handy and it prevented the total destruction of their trailer.

Pulling together a package of boat, motor and trailer for walleye fishing requires more than a casual inspection and a quick

34

decision. A quality boat, motor and trailer, if properly cared for during fishing season and during the winter months, will provide years of superb service. It's also a major investment, and just like buying a house or automobile, it requires more than a little thought.

Study various boats and motor combination. If possible, take them out onto the water before spending your money. If that isn't practical, spend time with a walleye pro and pick his brain.

Put considerable thought into the boat-motor-trailer decision before plunking down some deposit money. I've gone through many rigs over the past 15 years, and I know what I want under my feet when I take to the water.

Given enough thought, buying and rigging out a walleye boat that will meet your exacting needs and standards is easy. But, if you choose what looks good without giving thought to using it during calm and rough water conditions, you may have to live with a costly mistake.

Photo by Tony Sailer

 **35**

Boat Control

Make no mistake about it. Boat control, whether running forward or backward, is as important as the lure on the end of your line. Good boat control will put anglers on fish; poor control of your craft will keep fishermen from attaining optimum walleye catches.

Lake Erie waves during April 1995 tournament were 10 to 14 feet high.

What you are about to read are actual events that have happened on many occasions throughout the United States and Canada. Eight to 10-foot waves with 45 miles-per-hour wind gusts are extreme angling and boating conditions for even walleye pros, but they have happened often enough that anglers learn what to do and not to do when these conditions arise.

I would be remiss if I didn't offer a cautionary note. I would never advocate anyone fishing in such windy conditions, but Gary

Roach and I have done so many times, but we never recommend it to others.

Once a person has fished in heavy weather, doing so in waves of two to three feet is child's play. Actually, the average person can fish in weather like this without serious problem providing they know their boat and motor, know how to read wave conditions and can handle a boat.

With that in mind, here are some thoughts from my fishing partner Gary Roach and some of my thoughts.

BACK TROLLING

Photo by Tony Sailer

Gary Roach back trolling along a narrow rock reef while Mark Martin uses the bow mount for the same purpose.

This is a special form of boat control. By putting the motor in reverse an angler can troll backwards to follow certain structures at a specific depth and speed. This time-tested technique will improve your boat control and produce more fish than by aimlessly letting the boat drift with the wind.

It's a great method to use when walleyes are in deep water or have become tough to catch. This s-l-o-w approach offers more precise control and it allows fishermen to spend more time with bait or lure in key locations.

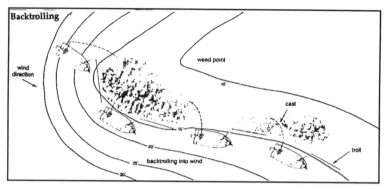

Courtesy of In-Fisherman

When back trolling, fishermen are more precise as they follow structure like reefs or dropoffs. It's possible to backtroll with jigs, Northland Roach Rigs or bottom bouncer rigs with much greater precision. Anglers also can cast to the shoreline or nearby structure with jigs or crankbaits while back trolling.

It's easy to stay on structure when using a motor on the back of the boat as the pivot point. The bow of the boat will follow wherever the stern goes.

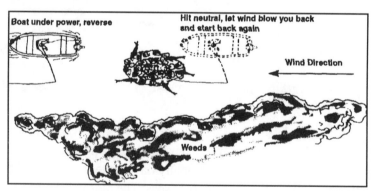

If you want the boat's bow straight on to or parallel to the bar or other structure, try using a boat brake or sea anchor. Tie it to the bow on a short rope so it won't tangle in the motor. This is especially helpful if you have a severe crosswind coming across your beam.

Back trolling is most often done into the wind but you can also back troll with the wind while using a sea anchor to slow your speed. It's possible to back troll in a river current.

One good example of backtrolling while river fishing is to position the boat above a wing dam and hold its position by back trolling along the front or upstream side. If the boat starts going too fast or going too far upstream from the intended target, kick the motor into neutral for a few seconds. This will slow the boat down or allow the current to push it closer to structure before reversing the motor again.

Try using a gas or electric motor to backtroll. Today's modern engines, like Motor Guide's electric models, have plenty of power for fishing in windy weather or heavy current.

When the wind really kicks up, or when we've got two to four-foot waves, Gary and I will use our Mariner "kicker" or our main outboard for additional control. Gary fishes from a Lund Tournament Series 2025 Pro-V with a 125 horsepower tiller motor while I use a 225 horsepower Mariner with a smaller 9.9 horsepower four stroke tiller motor with a TR-1 autopilot. Gary will also use his 36-volt bow- and stern-mounted trolling motors, depending on the wind and wave conditions.

My boat is a Lund 2025 Pro-V Deluxe with console steering rather than the tiller motor that some walleye anglers prefer. My Lund is custom designed with electric motors located in the front and back.

When I use the bow-mounted electric motor, I'm doing pretty much the same thing that Gary does while backtrolling. The boat is moving slowly and precisely along structure.

We both use precise boat control to stay on fish. A bow-mounted motor pulls the boat, exactly like a backtrolling engine, except that I move forward. Gary will occasionally have better boat control than I will, especially in four to five-foot seas. The reason is he has more power with a big 125 H.P. tiller gas engine, and his boat is designed specifically for backtrolling.

My preference is to use the bow-mounted electric or the TR-1 autopilot mounted on the 9.9 kicker.

At times I may have to work harder than Gary to keep on target but I find my bow system offers some advantages. For one thing, I have both hands free. One thing to remember with a bow-mounted

Photo by Dave Dulaney

Using the TR-1 to navigate from one fish icon to another.

engine is to make sure the shaft is long enough to stay in the water so it provides enough thrust to control the boat when working along good structure.

The TR-1 autopilot is a device that fits on the small kicker engine that has a built in compass and Gyro system and it allows me to have both hands free. When you point the bow of the boat where you want to go, turn the autopilot on forward. It works the same way when backtrolling except you point the stern towards the direction you want to go and push the reverse autopilot on. It also has the capabilities to interphase with your G.P.S. system. It has a cord remote system for intimate adjustments in course or even throttle control anywhere in the boat. This device has helped me do very well in many situations.

Anglers fishing from the bow may try filling the bow live well with water, and then move anchors and heavy tackle boxes forward to make everything slightly bow-heavy. Use a very short line on a sea-anchor off the bow cleat.

This extra weight and a sea-anchor will help keep the bow down in the water, making it easier to control and handle the boat. This method has worked very well for me while fishing the walleye tournament trail.

A loss of boat control means anglers must start rethinking the situation. You may have to work structure in heavy seas by starting upwind from the structure you plan to fish. Set up and allow the wind to help by blowing the boat along.

Photo by Al Kyser

Mike Trent and I stabilize front of boat as we move along a breakline and slow our pace with a sea anchor.

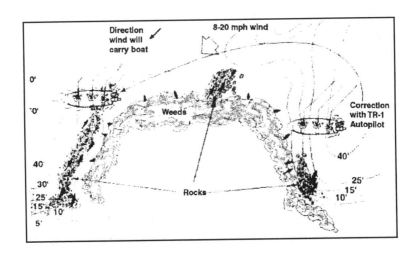

If you start drifting off-course or moving too fast, a simple burst of power into the wind will slow down the drift and put the boat back on structure and at the depth that was producing fish.

If the waves exceed four feet, start backtrolling with the main engine. Anglers will need the power of a big engine to go backwards. If you start moving too fast, put the engine into neutral for a few seconds, and then put it back into reverse to continue along the structure.

Even when front trolling with planer boards on big water like Lake Erie or Michigan's Saginaw Bay, it's possible to go too fast because of high winds and waves. In such conditions, try fishing with the wind because it will allow greater boat speed control. Whenever my boat speed becomes too fast, I shut down the kicker engine and allow the wind to move me at the right speed while steering with the big engine's skeg. If you're going too fast put a small sea anchor out on a short rope. This will help to slow you down.

If I'm long-line trolling at night or fishing along structure during the day, I use my electric motor to fish with the wind. Use the wind to position the boat and the electric motor to maintain speed and control. This method uses very little battery juice, certainly much less than when fishing into the wind.

When fishing into the wind, and when the electric motor doesn't have enough power or it is too much work to use the electric's foot control pedal, try firing up the gas kicker motor. Lock it into the straight-on position and put it into gear for added thrust.

Gary reminded me that once on South Dakota's Lake Oahe the wind was gusting to 45 miles per hour and almost everyone had quit fishing except us. We could still backtroll. Sure, we were getting wet but we were still fishing. In fact, I won that tournament and attribute my success to backtrolling in bad weather.

Fishermen don't always have to backtroll in rough water. It's possible to front troll by using a sea anchor off the bow to keep the boat from constantly swinging around in the wind.

Another advantage of a tiller motor is for quick reaction time in rough water. Trolling into or quartering into the wind requires con-

stant vigilance to control boat direction, and a simple tiller movement is easier and faster than turning a steering wheel.

When considering a bow-mounted electric motor, choose the shaft length carefully. A low-profile boat doesn't need a long shaft but a high, deep V design like my Lund requires a longer shaft, one over 54 inches in my case. A shaft that works well in calm water may mean that the prop will come out of the water on days with three to four-foot waves.

One accessory that virtually every professional walleye fisherman uses is the Wave Wacker. A Lund and other modern boats have a transom 20-25 inches high. Even a transom that high isn't enough to keep water from coming into the boat while backtrolling. Wave Wackers are a custom fitted shield that mounts on the transom on both sides of an outboard. They curl backwards to deflect waves that smack into the stern.

The design is cut out to fit around a kicker engine and electric motor. They won't help much with the occasional six-footer that crashes over the stern, but in everything else, they will keep you much drier.

Wave Wackers

Lund has really built a good name and reputation with their guide-tested boats. The Lund's hull design was developed by working with and listening to those fishermen who use them. That's why anglers see so many professional walleye pros use them in tournaments and do so well. It's the primary reason why so many fishing guides and lodges use them.

So, the next time walleye water starts calling, give our boat control methods a try. You'll find that more fish are caught with a slow presentation and precise boat control.

And those are pretty good reasons to learn what your boat and motor can do. Properly used, boat control provides a smoother ride, more fishing time, and more fish in the live well.

Photo by John Peterson
A successful day of fishing is the end result of proper boat control.

Read A Lake

In preceding chapters, the make-up of different types of North American lakes has been described. Fishermen who want to learn how to fish a lake should study this information and file it away for future reference. Sooner or later, a situation will arise when this knowledge can be used.

Fishermen who study a lake contour map, scratch their heads, head for a boat and then start catching fish are the envy of other anglers. Some guides can do it but it's usually on their "home" lake.

The people I really admire, however, are tournament fishermen who study a lake and then catch fish almost every time. Sure, they fish for dollars where the name of the game is catching fish. However, you can use their tricks to gain a greater insight into where fish are located. Here's how the pros do it.

The primary goal of most fishermen is to catch fish. They may enjoy jawboning with a buddy, watching a purple sunset, or seeing wildlife along a lakeshore; but the one driving force that puts people on the water is a burning desire to catch fish. The average fisherman wants the thrill of a fish tugging against a bowed rod, and he wants freshly fried fillets for dinner.

The trick to catching more fish — anywhere — is to learn to read the water whether it is a lake or stream. This doesn't require mystical powers or a palm reader's pointed hat. It just requires common sense, some knowledge of what to look for, and the ability to understand what you see.

The first step to becoming a skilled lake fisherman is to purchase a bottom contour (hydrographic) map of a lake you plan to fish. Hydrographic maps are available from many sources. Try Lake

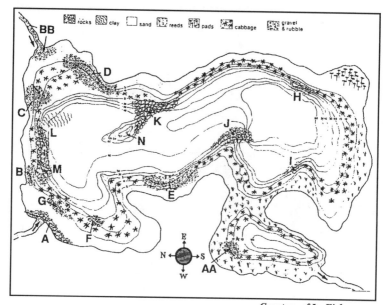

Courtesy of In-Fisherman

A typical hydrographic map keyed for fishing different areas during the year.

Survey Center, 630 Federal Office Building, Detroit, MI 48226 for Great Lakes waters; U.S. Army Engineers District Office, 906 Olive Street, St. Louis, MO 63101 for the Mississippi River and its tributaries (charts show some lakes); U. S. Geological Survey, Map Information Office, National Center, Reston, VA 22092; and Geological Survey, Department of Energy, Mines and Resources, 601 Booth Street, Ottawa, Ontario, Canada KlA OE9.

Fishermen can often find maps in limited quantities by writing to the Waterways or Fisheries Division of the Department of Natural Resources of the state, province or Canadian territory they want to fish.

Fishing Hot Spots, Inc. of Rhinelander, WI 54501, 1-800-338-5957, produces many maps of inland lakes that hold walleyes. Ask for specific maps or a catalog of their different products.

Study a map and locate areas where fish migrations are likely. These migration routes are the avenues gamefish follow from a deep-water sanctuary to shallow feeding zones. Pinpoint sharp or rounded

Photo by Tony Sailer
Randy Bandstra and Mark Martin studying a map to locate structure that may hold fish.

points that dead-end in deep water. Note close-together contour breaks, learn the locations of sunken islands or heavy weedbeds, determine where deep-water weedlines are located, and observe the exact depth of gravel areas or sunken stumps or boats. Any fish-bearing piece of structure found on these maps will put an angler one step ahead of others.

Along with good maps, fishermen should use a good fish finder and never take your eyes off it while searching for good looking structure. It puzzles me that so many people go fishing and use only their eyes to look for structure above and below the water.

I look at everything above the water, study hydro and topo maps, turn on my fish finder and start looking for fish. If I find some structure 100 feet long and 50 feet wide, and only see three fish, I'll keep going unless these are the only fish I've seen in the past hour. What gets my blood pumping is to see 10 or 15 fish on one structure. The more fish you find, the easier they are to catch. At times it will take an hour or two to find a spot with enough fish to make me want to start fishing. But who is to say they will all be walleyes.

They could be perch, bass, pike, bluegills and perhaps walleyes. Keep the sonar unit working as you fish, and visually scan the surroundings for other structure. This makes it easier to make a deci-

Photo by Tony Sailer
By studying contour maps and using a fish finder
Gary Roach and Mark Romanack hit paydirt.

sion whether to keep fishing or to try a different area.

This anecdote emphasizes the point that good fishing areas can be found before launching the boat. Weather conditions are always a factor, but given good weather, an angler can vastly increase his chances of an evening fish-fry by checking contour maps and then studying the lake. Many contour maps are outdated because of physical changes in a lake's surface or subsurface structure. Try to obtain the newest contour charts available.

Studying a lake visually and determining what treasures lie below isn't difficult, but it does take some work. A shimmering expanse of water captures the eye, and most people just mutter: "It looks good to me." The lake may hold plenty of fish or it may not; much depends on underwater structure. Most, but not all, underwater structure can be clearly seen by looking at the surrounding shoreline. Learn shoreline structure, and the underwater areas will take care of themselves. Everything will then fall into place, just like the pieces of a jigsaw puzzle.

Reading a lake from above water is not difficult. Keep in mind that roughly 90 percent of any lake contains no fish. The next fact should be obvious: only 10 percent of a lake has good fish-bearing structure. This means that regardless of how inviting a lakeshore

Photo by Roger E. Peterson

This walleye is cruising along structure.

appears, only a very small percentage of the available water contains fish. Anglers should learn to differentiate between scenic areas, and those that actually produce fish. There is a difference, as we shall soon see.

Walleyes need three basic things in their life: food, shelter and protection or comfort. A brief look at each should point anglers toward an easier analysis of fish-bearing structures, both above and below water.

FOOD

Walleyes feed on insect larva, plankton, minnows, small forage fish,

Photo by Roger E. Peterson

(L) A typical cold front walleye tight to bottom along structure.

49

Photo by Roger E. Peterson

Walleye cruising along structure loaded with crayfish.

crayfish, mollusks, or whatever else is available in a lake. They can go for several days after a cold front without food. This is one explanation for why we often encounter poor fishing.

Food must be immediately accessible to sportfish. Food is of little value to walleyes if they must spend the energy to swim a mile or two down a lake to an area where forage is present.

A general rule is that walleyes are found in areas where their food is located. An example would be a lake where crayfish are the primary food for smallmouth bass. We know that smallies eat crayfish, and we also understand that crayfish are not found everywhere in a lake. Good structure located near crayfish habitat should be a prime fishing area.

SHELTER

Gamefish "shelter" means different things to different gamefish species. For example, crappies will use a brushpile as shelter to hide from other predatory species. Shelter could also be a stump field, a maze of stickups, logjams, weedbeds, islands near deep water, a swimming raft anchored in deep water, or anything else that offers comfort or shelter to fish. It could be a point extending from the shallows into deep water, a jumble of boulders or ledgerock, or a

Photo by Roger E. Peterson
Walleye taking shelter next to log along structure.

spruce toppled into the water on a northern lake.

COMFORT OR PROTECTION

Comfort can mean many things whenever anglers refer to gamefish needs. It might be oxygen-rich waters or a water temperature that keeps forage fish and gamefish actively moving. It also refers to lake areas where fish can find protection.

Deep water is the sanctuary for many gamefish. Deep water usually offers the concealment larger members of a species need to protect themselves from overhead predation, the bright rays of the sun, and other factors including fishermen. Many lake fishermen are shoreline-oriented; they work the shallows, cast to lily-pad fields, and seldom heave their lures into deep water. They remind me of a stream steelhead fisherman afraid to fish near bottom for fear of getting snagged and losing his terminal rigging. Successful lake fishermen realize that bigger fish are usually found in deeper water. It's worth losing a few rigs to tangle with a possible trophy.

Fish those areas where fish have direct access to deep water. This doesn't mean fishing 100 or 200 yards away; position yourself no more than 10 or 20 feet from deep water. A frightened walleye's first response to danger is to go deep. We've all caught and released

51

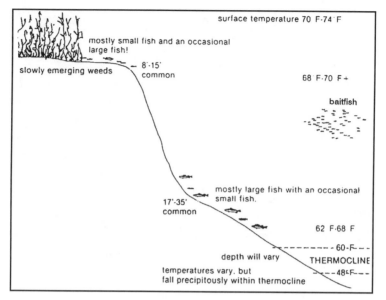

Courtesy of In-Fisherman

a fish. What does it do? It often swims in a dazed circle, gets straightened out, and heads for deep water. It's heading for comfort and protection.

WHAT TO LOOK FOR

A big tip-off to walleye activity on any lake is minnow life. Any area that supports good minnow populations near shoreline weeds or in offshore waters should offer first-rate walleye action.

What else should lake fishermen look for when trying to pinpoint hot fishing areas? The first thing I check on any lake is the shoreline. Is it flat, without a tapering shoreline leading into the water? If so, the lake probably is an old lake with a slow break into deep water. Fish will probably be in deep water much of the time, except during overcast days or at night.

Is the shoreline sharp, with many points or islands? If so, the water usually drops off rapidly from the first breakline. Good fishing can often be done near the islands or off points.

Is the shoreline extremely rocky, with sharp cliffs and vertical rock faces? Such waters usually are found on young lakes and indi-

Sharp drop off points

Photo by Denny Geurink

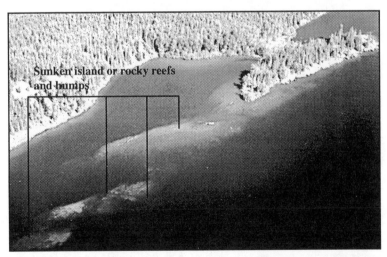

Sunken island or rocky reefs and humps

Photo by Denny Geurink

Cove or bay with rocks and weeds.

Rocky contour surrounding a small island.

A fish underwater
holding on structure

This photo was taken by using proper sunglasses and using a polarizing filter on my camera lens.

cate a rapid dropoff, often near shore. These lakes can be tough to fish, but not impossible to read. Walleyes are often found on sunken islands that come out of deep water to within 10- to 12-feet of the surface. Others are located in shallow bays with good underwater structure nearby, near in-flowing streams, or in pools cut by small waterfalls.

This is the first step to reading a lake. Learn to look at shoreline features. Common sense will tell you what bottom contours can be found away from shore.

The next step is to look carefully for fish-holding areas such as standing timber in impounded waters, small islands, rocky reefs that kick up waves when water washes over them during a stiff wind, sandbars, weedbeds, or underwater humps. These can be located on a contour chart, or by actual observation. The most difficult thing to observe from shore is an underwater hump.

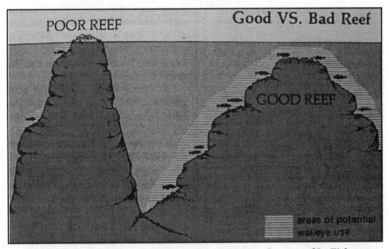

Courtesy of In-Fisherman

A baitshop owner can often pinpoint hump locations but they may also appear on a chart. Other types of structure can often be seen by looking for them, and this is where my Costa Del Mar polarized sunglasses come in handy. The important thing is to train your eyes and mind to look for structural changes.

Watch for shoreline features that could hold fish, and an easy one is a dock leading out into the lake. Are there boats anchored in deep water or a swimming raft? Is the shoreline indented with numerous coves, cuts, or small bayous, or is the shore straight and without visual structure?

Good fishing can often be had in small coves, especially in the spring. Use your nose to locate fish. I can't sniff out gamefish like some anglers, but I can detect a fishy odor in some locations.

Some anglers incorrectly associate this fishy smell with shallow water and decaying plant life. I used to think the same way until a

Concrete bridge abutments with current are good places to check out.

buddy told me that my long nose was smelling fish life. We caught many bluegills and some three-pound largemouth bass that day. I've since learned to fish in areas where such strong fishy odors are found.

Impoundments often have concrete piers, bridges, or causeways along or over the water. Small currents often form beneath such objects. This moving water can be a source of top-notch action. Never pass up an area with concrete abutments. They offer prime cover for most gamefish.

Does your favorite lake have an old creekbed, or does it feature an inlet, outlet or both? All will attract fish. Marshy waters near an inlet, or a delta near the outlet, may offer the finest fishing of the year, particularly in spring or fall if migratory species are found in the lake.

I've seen bass, pike, walleyes, muskies and even yellow perch make spawning runs there. The fishing, if seasons are open at the

Key areas to fish are edges of old creek or river beds next to old standing flooded timber.

time, can be terrific.

Does your favorite walleye lake have sandy beaches or a swimming area? These places are seldom productive during daylight hours but can deliver some fast action after sundown. They can be seen easily with the naked eye.

I've caught some big walleyes by fishing sinking lures at night, even in areas where people were swimming. The turbulence that swimmers create loosens plant life or plankton, and this attracts forage fish. Walleyes are usually close to an available food supply, and such areas are overlooked by many fishermen.

How far must a walleye or any other gamefish species swim from deep water before hitting the shallows of a beach where food is available? Swimming beaches usually have deep water within 50 yards of the shallows. A swimming raft, anchored in deep water, is held in place with cement blocks or other heavy material to prevent it from drifting away in high winds.

A walleye that moves into the shallows will often hold at the first break on structure. In this case it's probably the raft's cement blocks on bottom. The next step for the fish is to move up to the lip of the dropoff and then swim into the shallows to feed.

I used to wonder why swimming rafts often produce good walleye fishing. Now I know.

Photo by Rachael Martin

Paula Martin caught this walleye in a weedbed next to a swimming area.

Photo by Lanny Orvalla

Gary Roach, Mr. Walleye ®

Natural Lakes

Walleyes are one of North America's favorite gamefish. They are found in a variety of waters ranging from natural lakes to impoundments. Within each body of water are several factors that will usually dictate when, where and how to fish.

These varying types of water lead to different challenges for a walleye angler. Fishing techniques can vary from one lake to another, and often the methods used will be dictated by local structure, forage fish and/or weather conditions.

In order to fish each type of lake or impoundment, and do it properly, it's important to understand the specific characteristics that make them different. What follows is an in-depth look at some of those differences, and by understanding them, can be the difference between success or failure.

More walleyes are caught from natural lakes than impoundments. Impounded waters are not new, but the adding of walleyes to them is a fairly recent innovation for fisheries managers. With that in mind, we'll first look at what natural lakes offer and how that information can lead to better catches.

NATURAL LAKES:

Natural lakes are fairly abundant in North America. Often called seepage lakes, they are usually spring-fed, or fed by precipitation or groundwater runoff. If they contain sufficient mineral content and heavy weed cover, natural seepage lakes can hold almost any species of fish.

Natural lakes are often categorized by their age. There are oligotrophic (young) lakes; mesotrophic (middle-aged) lakes; and eutrophic (old) lakes. Let's examine each type in turn.

OLIGOTROPHIC (YOUNG) LAKES:

Picture yourself on a Canadian lake, preferably on a windswept point where ledgerock outcroppings are common and whiskey jays circle over your evening campfire. A white water stream crashes into one end of the lake and a shallow feeder stream connects that lake with another over a spruce-studded ridge. This, by our standards, is an oligotrophic lake. Lake trout, pike and walleyes, a few smallmouth bass, and whitefish probably inhabit this lake. These lakes are about 12,000 years old, young by geological standards.

A young lake is low in nutrients—those enriching factors that quickly age a lake. Oligotrophic lakes are rocky waters with exposed rock walls, large boulders or heavy ledge rock, and steep shorelines that are usually dotted with evergreens or birch.

Such steep-sided lakes have sharp dropoffs and little weed growth except in shallow, protected bays. Most oligotrophic lakes are deep, some are 100 feet or more in depth. Rocky reefs are fairly common, and often jut from the lake floor without any discernible pattern.

In the spring look for walleyes to be concentrated around creeks, rivers, small shallow bays and new emerging weeds. In early to late summer the best locations will be underwater reefs. The best presentations for this type of fishing are bottom bouncers with spinners. They allow you to cover more water along the reefs and

Photo by Denny Geurink

Photo by Paula Martin

Typical Oligotrophic (young) type of stream running between two lakes.

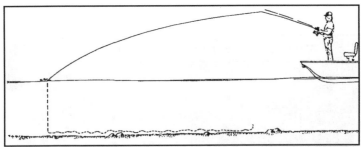

Twitch and drag method.   *Courtesy of In-Fisherman*

find active fish faster. You then can go back and pick up a few more in key locations with a slower approach with a jig or rig. Use your fish finder because not all reefs will hold populations of fish.

My favorites are main lake points along dropoffs and weedbeds along sandy bays. In these areas especially along lake points use bottom bouncers and spinners along the weedbeds. Pitch jigs or cast crankbaits like ShadRaps or countdown Rapalas. Early in the spring a twitch and drag method may entice inactive walleyes to hit.

Food supplies for gamefish are scarce. Many lakes of this type are found along the Canadian border.

I remember many times in early June catching walleye, whitefish, northern pike, and lake trout in this type of lake. I would fish the boulder strewn shoreline structure from five to 12 feet deep.

MESOTROPHIC (MIDDLE AGE) LAKE

We'll switch locations now, to a lake in northern Michigan. The broken-rock shoreline shows a more gradual taper and is a mix of hardwoods and pine. Shallow coves may contain weeds in quiet areas, while heavy weed growth is often found along the first dropoff. This is a mesotrophic lake, and it is common throughout the United States.

A mesotrophic lake is a fertile body of water that can support large populations of trout, largemouth bass, smallmouth bass, panfish, walleyes, northern pike, muskies, and other gamefish. Such lakes can be deep or shallow. A thermocline often forms in deeper waters. When this happens you can see the thermocline on your graph and also locate schools of fish. Get out your In-Line planer boards and set crankbaits or bottom bouncers and spinners just above the schools

A good walleye location is a sandy beach with cabbage weeds on a Mesotrophic Lake.

of fish. Get ready for you could possibly find some great action. Some lakes do not develop a thermocline, although another nearby meso lake will. It seems to be an unstable characteristic of this age-class of lakes.

The physical characteristics of a mesotrophic lake vary from one area to another. The lakes have typical rock outcropping in some areas, although these tend not to be as sharp-featured as they are in oligotrophic lakes.

The shoreline of a mesotrophic lake is often bordered by rocks. The nearby forest consists of hardwoods predominantly, although pines exist in some areas. Weed growth is usually found in shallow water, while cabbage weeds are often present in deeper water. Where this happens break out the jigs and crankbaits. Start pitching jigs and casting cranks, you might find some walleyes this way. The dropoff is usually a long, slow taper down to mid-depths. This is followed by a steep drop down to bottom. The floor of many lakes is often a buildup of sediment and decomposed materials. Look for walleyes in the same areas as I explained in the Oligotrophic Lakes and use the above techniques.

During July and August be prepared to go deep on these bodies of water and use your graph to find the sunken reefs and long tapering points. Check these long tapering points out to deep water, and any water from 15 to 35 feet should be checked out thoroughly.

EUTROPHIC (OLD) LAKES

Let's take a speedy cross-country trip and look at a typical eutrophic lake. This one is in the South, but eutrophic lakes are found throughout the country. Location makes little difference in the aging process of a lake.

This Florida lake is shallow and weed-filled; the surrounding terrain is flat. Trees are often sparse along shore, and the water sits on a soft or mucky bottom. Thin reed beds may be found along the banks, and aquatic vegetation often grows from the lake floor to the surface.

Bass, pickerel, and some panfish are common. If the lake is really old and located in the North, it will support populations of carp or bullheads. If it's a southern lake, it will hold trash fish. Sediment has filled in spawning sites, and oxygen depletion has killed many species.

Such waters are usually rich in nutrients either man-made or natural. Weed growth and algae, or "bloom," can cover much of the lake's surface and blot out most of the life-giving oxygen.

Early eutrophic lakes are capable of sustaining good fishing. Waters are often warm and contain weeds rooted to the bottom. This weed growth often extends from the shallows down to a depth of 18 or 20 feet. Eutrophic lakes are typified by shallow water and flat or semi-flat terrain. Lakeside hardwoods, such as oak and maple, are common in many sections of the country.

A deep eutrophic lake is capable of forming a thermocline, but as the lake continues to age and fills up with sediment, this fish-producing band of water ceases to exist.

Dropoffs, as stated before, are slow and gradual. Points are usually rounded and fairly shallow. Large flats are often covered with just a few feet of water. Most are muck-bottomed and devoid of fish life. Some lakes have sunken islands or above-water islands still rooted to bottom. These areas often produce fair-to-good fishing.

An angler should determine the type of lake he's fishing before he begins. The next step is to determine the types of structure present in the lake. For instance, does the lake have shallow or medium-depth weeds? These areas can be good early or late in the day, or after dark.

What do shallow-water flats offer? If some sand grass or weeds are available with a slight dropoff to deeper water, they can be hotspots at night for walleyes, although good fishing can be had during daylight hours in dark-colored water. Such areas are usually best during summer months. At what depth are the deep weeds and the deep-water weedlines located? If it's six to 12-feet, great. What type of weeds are present? Cabbage and coontail for sure, with a little sand

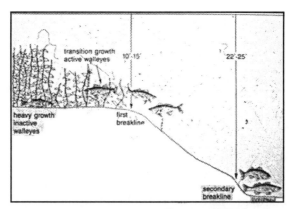

Courtesy of In-Fisherman

grass and a good growth of cabbage or coontial is just fine. These questions, when answered, will determine where you find fish on dark or sunny days. A bright day usually will attract walleyes to the deep-water edge of weeds, often in 15 to 20 feet of water. They usually show little interest in lures, and many may be half-buried in weeds. Overcast skies or periods of darkness may spur these fish to visit the shallow-water edge of the weedbeds. A good movement will find fish moving up onto the flats, and into the shallows to feed.

Analyze whether the lake has a lip of clean bottom, and the length of this lip. This can be an excellent food shelf and a good place to run a bottom bouncer and spinner to find active fish. This stretch can be any length and is a continuation of the gradual or quick taper of the bottom contours. It extends normally from the deepest point of the weedline down to the first major breakline or dropoff into deep water. It's common for walleyes to travel and feed heavily along this lip if forage fish are present.

At what depth does the first major dropoff occur? Usually 10- to 12 feet. This dropoff can show a bottom of muck, sand, gravel, rocks, boulders, or any combination of these materials. Walleyes often hold along this first dropoff if a thermocline is present. Such areas offer cooler water and abundant forage. The steepness of the breakline may determine the species of fish present, but don't count on it. I've seen walleyes and smallmouth bass using such a breakline. Then, ten casts later, I'll catch a cruising northern pike. (It doesn't take a big stick with a lot of knots in it to pound some sense into my head.)

If you pick up one species of fish, and then catch another species that is uncommon to that particular stretch of water, it's just possible that a very good fish movement is underway. Stick with it and count your blessings. I can tell you that steeper breaks are good early and late in the year while gradual tapers are good during summer time.

Is there a secondary dropoff or breakline? If so, at what depth is it found? One spot where I take big walleyes often is along a secondary breakline. This location seems to attract the really large fish during hot summer months in mesotrophic lakes. Such dropoffs may have inward or outward breaks (called cups), and gamefish are attracted to these areas. I've seen several cases where small schools of big walleyes will suspend just off the secondary breakline. These fish can be taken regularly by a Northland Roach Rig using a floating jig-head and crawler or leech or a Northland Bottom Bouncer with a long snell with a bead and hook set up.

What is the bottom content? We've just learned that mucky bottoms are found on eutrophic lakes, combination bottoms on mesotrophic lakes, and hard, rocky bottoms on oligotrophic lakes. The character preferences of various groups of walleyes will determine whether they are strict bottom dwellers or not. Most species will spend some time near the floor of a lake, but will often associate themselves with some type of structure along breaklines or be suspended. Finding fish on breaklines may be more time consuming, but once found, they are usually easier to catch.

These simple keys should help you learn the potential of any given lake. Practice will enable you to spot character differences between lakes just by driving past them. It's not necessary to fish a body of water to recognize which of the three categories it fits into.

SHIELD LAKES

The border waters between the United States and Midwestern Canada offer a different breed of natural lake. A "shield" lake is a fragile body of water located on or along the Canadian or Precambrian Shield, a band of rocky terrain stretching across northern North America. These waters are located in areas where nutrient-producing sediment or rock layers have eroded away in the lake basin and in nearby terrain. These lakes support cold water gamefish such as

Shield Lake   *Photo by Paula Martin*

smallmouth bass, lake trout, whitefish, walleyes, and some northern pike. Shield lakes are excellent fish habitats. Many are found in wilderness areas.

The Canadian Shield contains the rock formations common to shield lakes. This shield area encompasses most of Ontario, all of Quebec, parts of Manitoba and Saskatchewan, the eastern two-thirds the Northwest Territories, all of Labrador, and small portions of northern Michigan, Wisconsin, Minnesota, and North Dakota. Lakes found within this region are wilderness gems—rough-cut diamonds amid a sea of spruce. Clean waters sparkle, and fishing is generally good.

There are two types of shield lakes: a large lake with little deep water over 40 feet, or a lake with much deeper water. The former is typically a walleye haven.

These shield lakes are usually oligotrophic waters. Shorelines are made up of boulders, ledgerock, gravel, and rubble. Sand is not common in this area, (however, if sand is found, fish it, sand seems to be a magical breakline) nor are muck-bottomed lakes or mucky land. If muck is located nearby, even within this particular shield area, it isn't a shield lake. The water qualities are soft, containing few minerals and the lakes are infertile, supporting little vegetation.

Shield lakes usually remain cool during the summer while other nearby oligotrophic lakes warm up. Cool water prevents the growth of algae, which in turn retards the minnow population in a lake,

This shoreline is not a good place to fish shallow. There are no fist-size rocks to act as structure to hold bait fish.

increasing the competition for food among adult gamefish in shallow water. When gamefish have to compete for food, they often tend to concentrate in certain areas of a lake.

Many shield lakes are rich in dissolved oxygen, which enables deep-water species such as whitefish or lake trout to live in the depths all summer. These gamefish can either suspend over deep water or hold on or near bottom.

Gamefish found within shield lakes are often easier to catch than the same species found in more southern waters. Northern waters are relatively infertile, and food competition is keen. Crayfish, small minnows, and insects are the basic forage material for smallmouth bass and walleyes in shield lakes. Lake trout often feed on cisco. Growth is slow among gamefish, and it may take a smallmouth bass eight years to reach a 15-inch length.

Walleyes and smallmouth bass often use fairly shallow water (6- to 8-foot depths) to travel from one area to another. They seldom travel far just to locate food, however. Shield-lake gamefish move very little for food-gathering purposes due to the shortage of available munchies. Good spots to look for these gamefish include boulder-covered bottom areas in water less than 20 feet deep (although shield walleyes will hold in deeper water); any section of the lake that has a creek-fed cove or bay with several underwater structures nearby

This is an excellent place to fish shallow with wind and waves blowing in on rocks. If calm a good place to fish deep off shore.

(like rock piles, reefs, boulders, gravel, islands, and lip areas); or submerged logs and fist-sized boulders close to shore that also taper out into the deeper water. Look for islands that are rimmed with fist sized boulders instead of ledgerock. Sunken islands are a good choice from midsummer to early fall, as are long, broad points that extend out into the lake from an island. The latter choice is good most of the year. These locations generally produce good walleye catches.

Some structure locations in shield lakes are more important during one period than during others. Much depends on whether the angler is fishing during the prespawn, spawn, or postspawn period. Habitat preferences can differ from one group of walleyes to another.

Photo by Mark Pushneck

Mark Martin

Impoundments

Impoundments are fertile fish factories.

An impounded body of water can be divided into six major types: lowland, flatland, hill-land, highland, canyon, and plateau (depending on the nature of the surrounding environment). Each has one common denominator: all are dammed at the lower end of a stream, river or connecting waterway. The waters back up, flood the old stream channel, overflow into surrounding countryside, and create a fertile body of water with fast fish growth and good forage possibilities.

Walleyes are a popular gamefish, and they find their way through plantings or natural progression from the river, and many large southern and western lakes have been planted with these fish. And ... they wax fat and sassy on abundant forage fish.

It's entirely possible for anglers to learn the characteristics of one impoundment, travel a short distance, and discover a new and vastly different type of water in the next impoundment they fish. Bottom configurations differ from one to another, and fishing techniques can vary widely. An angler who is a "one-method fisherman" will pull his hair, rant and rave, and go fishless when trying new waters. Impoundments can be so different that methods that work in one place may be totally useless in another area.

To be successful, an angler must understand the differences among the six basic types of impoundments. Surrounding terrain gives the first clue to impoundment type. If flatland surrounds the impoundment, then it's probably a "flatland" impoundment. If mountain ranges tower overhead and the impoundment is in a canyon, it's a canyon-type impoundment. The other classifications are almost as easy to categorize. Shape of the impoundment, and surrounding countryside, are keys to easy identification.

Impoundments, regardless of type, can be deep, semi-deep, or shallow bodies of water. The depths of hill-land impoundments can fluctuate greatly.

Most of the impoundments discussed in this chapter will be fairly large bodies of water with at least 1,000 surface acres at pool stage. Many waters of this size already exist, and more are being built yearly. Large areas like this enable forage fish to reproduce. This, in turn, allow gamefish to grow quickly on abundant feed. Most impoundments are fertile during the first ten years of life. Thereafter, they maintain a steady level of fish productivity, although at a pace somewhat slower than during their formative years. Let's take an in-depth look at various characteristics found in the six types of impoundments. Understanding the differences can make a big difference in how many walleyes the angler may catch.

HILL-LAND IMPOUNDMENTS

This type of impoundment is very widespread, and is one of the toughest to read. It offers water ranging from weed-filled shallows to depths of 60 feet or more. Some hill-land impoundments can be more than 150 feet deep, and depths are determined by surrounding terrain. Hill-land impoundments have weedbeds, submerged and emergent timber, humps, flats, sharp breaklines, a river channel with numerous feeder streams, old roads, points, cemeteries, coves, and other structure elements. A hill-land impoundment normally has all these features, although some may possess only a few.

The upper end of the lake is usually shallow, with a flat bottom contour. The lower portion of the impoundment is deeper, and possesses a sharper shoreline.

River channels are normally located somewhere in the center portion of the lake. The old riverbed is straight. The river channel edges usually have steep sides that provide good cover and dark areas for resting fish.

Points are favorite locations for anglers seeking walleyes. Hill-land impoundments have rounded points that can be quite steep in the mid-depth or the deeper parts of the lake. Even shallow hill-land lakes have rounded points, although I've had little success taking fish from these areas, except in nearby deep water .

Coves found in the upper portions are usually moderately deep, while coves in the downstream areas are generally deeper. Dropoffs are more rapid in this lake-type than in a flatland reservoir. The water usually drops off rapidly from shore into about 10 or 12 feet of water before the depth-decline tapers off. So ... look for water that drops off fast, and then levels out to a fairly smooth lake floor.

Hill-land impoundments are usually weedy, especially in southern regions. Heavy weed growth provides abundant cover for forage fish and hiding places for bigger species. It also helps cool the water in hot-weather months. Southern impoundments usually feature stick-ups—cypress or pin-oak trees that emerge through the surface. Root sections or submerged branches are good spots to fish.

A long, tapering point with sand, gravel or shale are good spots to look for walleyes. Brush dots the shoreline (as shown in the above photo) and I've taken walleyes adjacent to the brush. Stick-ups at the ends of points can be a hotspot for feeding walleyes.

The one factor indicative of hill-land reservoirs is lots of structure. An angler may be fishing the old river channel for walleyes during a cold front or shallow covers during the prespawn or spawning period. Submerged timber provides attractive cover for gamefish, as does an abundance of other structure types.

FLATLAND IMPOUNDMENTS

Flatland impoundments are fairly common in the eastern two-thirds of the nation. These reservoirs are often surrounded by farmlands, and are usually shallow with 20-foot depths the average.

Such impoundments are primarily waterflooded farmland. Long flats are common, but steep dropoffs and underwater humps are unusual. Small islands can exist in these lakes, although some islands are more like medium-height hills or humps that rise above the surface from the middle of the lake.

Flood control was a major concern when flatland impoundments were built. Levees and dikes were common long before the lake filled, and these areas, along with the river and its feeder streams or oxbows, form the most structure in a flatland reservoir.

River channels can be straight or crooked. Some channel straightening is evident in many reservoirs. Ditches that were once used for rainwater runoff are common, and if they connect with an old riverbed, an angler can often enjoy good walleye action.

Oxbows are relatively new channels cut by a meandering current or by a flooding river. These locations are often found in otherwise flat ground. They can deliver a spectacular brand of action. Walleyes that spread out after the reservoir reaches pool stage often find sanctuary in deep oxbow cuts. Good vegetation is usually found near oxbows or the levees directly above them. A dike that parallels an oxbow can represent a breakline for fish migrating into the shallows to feed. Many levees were planted with bushes and shrubs to hold the soil in place before the lake was filled. Willows are common in many areas. The deep-water edge of these shrubs represent good fish cover in a flatland reservoir. Working jigs or bottom bouncers with spinners attached work especially well along these shrubs when the water is just a little more dingy than clear.

Points on flatland reservoirs are rounded, and may extend far out into the lake. Some points are brush-covered but they contain few trees. Such points are fairly shallow and offer good fishing only when found near the old river channel, a dike or levee, or an oxbow

with slightly deeper water and structure nearby.

Flatland impoundments have shallow coves. Some have small streams flowing into them, and weedbeds are quite common, The cover configuration depends on what the land looked like before it was covered with water. Coves with feeder streams can be walleye hotspots if the angler can locate structure leading from the deeper creek channel to the main riverbed or up onto other structure.

Photo by Jay Edwards

This walleye was caught in a deep creek channel next to a sand and shale point.

One type of structure common in many flatland reservoirs is an old road or causeway used by the state or landowner before flooding. Most roadways were slightly elevated, with a ditch on each side. Trees often lined these roads, and the ditch, brush, and trees are excellent fish producers.

Causeways were built across flatland impoundments to carry the load of vehicular or railroad traffic. Surrounding water near a causeway is usually shallow except where the old river channel passes beneath the bridge. Concrete bridge or causeway abutments located near deep water often attract feeding fish.

Other good structure on flatland lakes includes old buildings, basements where farmhouses were razed, small ponds that once were connected to the river, and riprap. The latter is often made of concrete chunks, placed years ago to help contain high water during river floodings. Gamefish often feed near riprap, and it is should never be overlooked by walleye fishermen.

LOWLAND IMPOUNDMENTS

Rip rap shoreline

It's commonly thought that lowland impoundments are found only in the South. Some of the top Wisconsin muskie waters, known locally as flowages, are really lowland impoundments. And besides producing muskies, many offer superb sport for walleyes as well. Many lowland reservoirs are in the South, but they also are common in the Midwest. Some anglers have never learned how to categorize these waters properly.

A lowland reservoir receives its name from its surroundings. Such impoundments are located near low, swampy terrain. In Michigan or Wisconsin, it might be a tamarack swamp tamed to supply electricity through a local power company. Bond Falls Flowage, in the northwestern Upper Michigan, is a classic example. It contains northern pike, muskies, walleyes, smallmouth bass, and other species. A drawdown of the lake during high energy use or little rain can reveal huge marl beds.

Good places to fish these waters are along and in the dead trees that line the shoreline or river arm. Work the jig from bottom to the surface using weedless jigs tipped with a crawler, leech or a minnow flipped out among the trees and branches. Fish may be anywhere in the brush. Another method is using a bobber and a jig placed in the cover as you dabble your other offering in and out of the pockets. Channels leading between lakes and backwater areas can collect quite a few walleyes. Every floating bog type of cover holds fish around and under it.

A southern lowland impoundment is often nothing more than a

Photo by Dan Donarski

Fallen trees and brush makes a typical spot to encounter walleye.

Photo by Doug Stamm

Walleyes located in the underwater trees and brush.

dammed swamp that allow water to spread over a large area. Many half-submerged tamarack or cypress trees, depending upon the area, were flooded. Fish inhabit the timbered edges, the old river channel, or small feeder streams that drain a marsh or swamp.

Lowland waters vary widely in depth. I've fished some 25- to 50-foot depths on northern lakes and longed to find 10-foot depths on some southern reservoirs. A dropoff from 8 to 10 feet can provide needed sanctuary for southern walleyes, while fish from northern Wisconsin may move from 25- to 10-foot depths during a shoreward feeding migration.

CANYON IMPOUNDMENTS

Photo by Dr. Tom Johnson

Canyon impoundments are relatively recent structures built for many reasons. Anglers are interested solely in the ability of a reservoir to produce fish, but such lakes were not constructed just for fishing. Many were built to provide an economical source of electricity or to harness the runaway powers of raging streams during spring floods.

Canyon-type reservoirs are the deepest impoundments. They often provide majestic western scenery, where most canyon impoundments are located. Many canyon lakes provide a two-story fishery, with warm water gamefish like bass or walleyes in the shallower depths, and trout in the lower levels. This type appeals to anglers because of its stark, rocky beauty and good fishing. Good forage is available, and rapid fish growth is common.

Such lakes are always dammed up by huge concrete dams that are usually located in narrow gorges. Towering walls and steep dropoffs are common. Such lakes contain very little vegetation except in some shallow coves, and most have clear water and good visibility. Both are assets for angler and gamefish.

Deep water is common in canyon lakes. It's not uncommon to find 100-foot dropoffs near shore, and depths of 500 feet or more are not unheard of. Much of this water isn't fully utilized by gamefish. Straining water this deep for walleyes can be a trying experience. Fortunately, anglers can usually find better action in much shallower depths.

Canyon lakes are often found in some of the most spectacular scenic areas in North America. Lake Powell in Arizona and Utah is stark, but its rugged beauty belies the fact that fantastic fishing can be had amid its sheer rock walls and deep side canyons. I fished with Tom Johnson on Wyoming's Boysen Lake for walleyes during the Governor's Cup Tournament in 1993, and did very well with a second-place finish. I count the experience of fishing a canyon reservoir like Boysen Lake as one of life's great pleasures.

Photo by Dr. Tom Johnson

The shoreline of most canyon reservoirs is comprised of steep cliffs, some over 1,000 feet high. Overhanging ledges can block the sun and provide cool, shaded places to fish. Such areas also attract gamefish trying to avoid direct sun rays. Broken rock faces that tumble down steep cliffs can form an erratic

 **81**

shoreline of boulders, rock slides, and ledges. This is the type of structure that has produced many walleyes for me in the past using bottom bouncers or jigs. Boulders that bounce off rock walls and crash into the water can form breaklines or breaks on structure leading from deep to shallow-water feeding zones. Fish use such areas regularly as they move inshore to feed.

Upper portions of a canyon reservoir may be less steep along the shoreline. Some lakes have mesas formed by a tapering rock wall face that is smooth and rounded—a steady attraction for trout and walleye.

Canyon reservoirs are often narrow. Some are over 100 miles long and contain many long, narrow coves. Many turns, bends, and arms feed the main lake. Tributaries often enter feeder arms and some may have several creeks emptying into the lake. Most coves are narrow and pointed, although a few are flat. Vegetation is sparse in most canyon impoundments because weeds can't grow although sagebrush may be found in the lake for a year or two after the water reaches pool stage.

Photo by Dr. Tom Johnson
The above picture shows low water conditions in a cove or bay, not a good place to fish. Fish when high water is near or above the brush or tree line.

Cottonwood or mountain cedars are fairly common in the extreme ends of coves. There is little out-of-water structure or vegetation to block sunlight, except for the sheer rock cliff walls. The water is often clear, with good visibility down to 50 feet.

An angler tasting the pleasures of a canyon-type lake can be awed by the beauty but overwhelmed by where to fish. It all looks good; structure other than riverbeds, feeder channels, broken rock formation, and sheer rock cliffs are seldom present.

One secret to fishing this type of water is to find areas out of the sun. I've taken walleyes from back bays to main points on these reservoirs. Some fish are caught by jigging steep rock faces that fall into 100 feet of water. A jumble of fallen rock that would be called riprap in other reservoirs often provides top fishing.

Shadowed areas in early morning or late afternoon can produce fast action if the angler is in the right place at the right time. Many hotspot can be 10 or 15 miles up or down the canyon. Running time cuts down on fishing time and success. Plan your most productive hours to coincide with your arrival in a good fish-producing location.

Photo by Paula Martin

Rising water: fish back bay points. Falling water: fish main lake points.

Many western anglers have this shadow business down pat. They fish eastern canyon walls in the morning, western walls in the afternoon, and take it easy during midday.

PLATEAU IMPOUNDMENTS

Plateau impoundments are usually found in Midwestern North America, but can be found right up to the Rocky Mountains. Irrigation of farm crops was the major reason for building most of these lakes,

Gary Roach pulling bottom bouncer and spinner along brush and mudline.

and they receive a large volume of water daily. Much of it is backed up by dams and the water levels can fluctuate which can affect gamefish.

Plateau reservoirs are large. Depths range from 50 to 200 feet. The surrounding terrain is quite flat. All waters drain naturally from the up-lake areas to the dam. Spring runoff can create heavy siltation as sediment settles and ruins previously good areas.

The plateau basin maintains a steady gradient from headwaters down to the dam. Sharp dropoffs, and rapid underwater structure changes, are uncommon. The river channel is usually straight, and follows the center of the reservoir. Riverbeds are normally flat, although the tops of the channel edges are distinctly rounded. Vegetation is sparse, and generally limited to small trees and some brush left behind by rising water. A drawdown often reveals brush near creek channel

The underwater structure between the island and main land point is called a saddle. This area is worth checking out.

and they are productive.

Coves are flat and wide-mouthed where they enter the main lake.

Some coves contain one or more feeder streams. Anglers can learn to read these coves by checking out the shoreline. A steep-edged cove normally has some deep water near shore while a flat-sided cove is normally flat-bottomed and relatively shallow. Both can be good spots to fish, depending on the season, and whether the

Brush in and along the creek channel at the back of a cove can be dynamite fishing during high water.

Gary Roach fishing the edge of a mud line into a cup that leads out to-wards a point of land with a mud line and around into another cup to the left.

 **85**

Steep banks containing sand, gravel and shale falling away to the lake shoreline along with a great mud line is a good spot to checkout for fish.

water is rising or falling.

Erosion is fairly common in plateau reservoirs. The forces of water eroding a sloping bank can provide shallow cups near shore that can offer good fishing all season especially when there is wind blowing into them. These cups often extend down into deep water because most of the erosion occurs when the lake is at low pool. Once the lake fills again these cups will hold fish. Above-water terrain will often show signs of erosion, and will indicate that such structure is found underwater.

Moderately steep banks are found along shore of some plateau impoundments. Such areas can produce good fishing and are worth exploring. They can be spotted by steep-sided hills falling away to the lake's shoreline if they contain sand, gravel and a shale makeup.

HIGHLAND IMPOUNDMENTS

Highland reservoirs are common in the east. A few examples would include Dale Hollow or Percy Priest reservoirs in Tennessee, Lake Ouachita in Arkansas, Lake Sidney Lanier in Georgia, and Table Rock, Norfolk and Greers Ferry on the Missouri-Arkansas border.

These lakes are the result of a foothill stream being dammed. Such low-mountain areas are common in Kentucky, Tennessee, Georgia, South Carolina, Arkansas, Missouri, and California. Impoundments like these are found in the foothills of southeastern mountain ranges and are characterized by steep banks, clear water, and rocky outcropping. Dale Hollow Reservoir on the Tennessee-Kentucky border is a typical highland impoundment, and it holds some huge walleyes.

My experience with highland impoundments dates back to 1982 when I first fished Greers Ferry in Arkansas. It was early March during a slight warming spell, and there was some runoff from small feeder creeks. The walleyes were staging in and around the creeks and rivers. I looked at my topo map of the impoundment and picked the shortest and the most wide open creek arm. I figured the sun would help warm the water and trigger spawning runs. We caught six fish that day from 6 to over 13 1/2-pounds.

The underwater structure found here includes sharp dropoffs and sloping shoreline banks covered with timber. I've taken walleyes many times in 2 to 6-feet of water near brush growing on slow tapering points consisting of sand, gravel and shale while fishing Greers Ferry, Norfolk and Lake Quachita in March and April. A slight dingy color or stain to the water is needed for a good daytime bite.

Highland reservoirs are often "two-story" lakes with trout in the cool depths and striped bass, smallmouth bass, largemouth bass, and muskies or walleyes in slightly warmer water. These lakes are picturesque, although not in the rugged sense of a canyon impoundment. Most highland lakes have several marinas along their shores but little other habitation. Most mountain people were removed (some, unfortunately, by force) when the Tennessee Valley Authority began their systematic construction of dams.

Steep, rocky points are common on highland lakes. They often taper well out into the lake, with sharp dropoffs near the tip. Many coves are long and pointed with one or more streams flowing into the main lake. Steep-sided walls can be found in the inlet areas, although some lakes have sharp wooded cliffs that fall into the water where rocks and small boulders provide fish cove. Rocky ledges are common near shore, and stair-stepping ledges often drop off within casting distance of the beach. Such areas are excellent spots for planer board use. Attach lines with crankbaits to a planer board and work them tight to the ledge edges.

Mossy or weedy areas are not common, except in the back portions of some coves. Many narrow coves open up on the back side, and deep water near shore is common, except where shorelines are flat and trees can grow. Flooded brushpiles are common in more hilly terrain.

Good spots during hot weather are deep channels that run from feeder arms out into the main lake. Such areas, especially near long points or around islands, are good.

Impounded waters aren't new. But few lake fishermen realize that impoundments can be very different, both above and below water. Structures are different. Walleyes react differently in some impoundments than in others (although all still have the same needs and preferences).

Techniques that work in one type of impoundment will probably work in another if the angler realizes the differences in structure, where fish hold and feed, and why they do so. Everything in lake fishing is related to structure. Learn the structure differences in each lake, and you'll be on the road to becoming a fishing star.

Several questions to ask a person familiar with the impoundment are: Is the water rising or falling? In rising water you'll find more fish on points or structure in the back bays. In falling water, the fish will usually pull out of the back bays and be on the main points leading into the main lake or riverbed. Another good spot is just inside a main lake point.

Pay attention to mud lines created by waves splashing across a point or the shoreline. That in itself creates a edge where dirty meets clear water. When you look at point edges and other structure with a mud line, fish the edge of the mud line along structure. Hang on to your fishing rod because fishing could become very exciting!

COMBINATION IMPOUNDMENTS

Some impounded waters contain features from some of the above impoundments. Rainey Lake in northern Minnesota and western Ontario is a classic example. It has some features of a canyon, hill-land and plateau impoundment.

In 1990, I fished in Ontario's Rainy Lake for walleyes. It was late in August, and clear skies had settled into the area for several days. The weather was mild -- just right for a full day of fishing.

We tried several supposedly hot areas for walleyes, but fishing seemed unseasonably slow. It took two full days before we found good concentrations of fish. One rocky island had a lip of submerged rocks, boulders, and rubble that jutted from the top of the reef in the 20- 25 depth to 65 feet. We found our fish along the top of the reef.

My wife Paula mentioned that she overheard people talking about

Photo By Roger E. Peterson

 **89**

Blueberry Island. When we pulled out the map we found it was one and a half miles from our position. We headed for the island but never got there. I was watching my graph and noticed that the bottom rose sharply from 110 to 10 feet, and immediately fell back down. We turned back over the shallow area and started seeing fish on the graph.

Paula was using a Roach Rig with an inflated crawler and she dropped it to bottom and immediately caught a 23-inch walleye. We then landed a 24 and 21-inch walleye.

This was a practice run for the In-Fisherman P.W.T. Championship. Not wanting other tournament fishermen to see us catching fish in this spot we decided to leave.

We were preparing to leave when a boat came toward us. It was my good friend and fishing partner Gary Roach. He asked how we were doing, and I told him.

He wanted to know how we found his No. 1 spot because it wasn't marked on any map.

However, seeing as how I beat him to it he told me it was mine

for the tournament. The rest is history because I won the First P.W.T. Championship held proving it was the No. 1 hotspot on the lake.

Photo by Gary Roach

Rivers

Running water is a walleye magnet.

Rivers and streams; deep water or shallow; free-flowing or a dam-controlled flow; man-made or natural streams; rocky bottom or sand; fast flowing or slow; walleyes love running water, and anglers who haven't learned this basic fact are missing a good bet.

Photo by Paula Martin
Muskegon River

I cut my walleye angling teeth at an early age on Michigan's Muskegon Lake. That drowned rivermouth lake is served by the Muskegon River, and walleyes are found from one end of it to the other, and many different types of water conditions are found in the lake and river.

Almost every angler worthy of being called a walleye fisherman has fished Canada at one time or another. Many lakes in Ontario,

Quebec, Manitoba and Saskatchewan are connected by free-flowing streams. Most are rocky with periodic stretches of fast water with deep holes, and most of these areas hold walleyes.

Fishermen who have tried their luck in such areas usually come away happy. Walleyes are plentiful in most Canadian rivers and streams, and they are willing biters. These fish, quite unsophisticated at times, usually can be caught readily.

Typical Canadian River *Photo by Paula Martin*

Anglers know that certain spots in Canadian streams hold fish. The walleyes seldom hold in fast water, but the first quiet water above or below a fast flowing riffle is a good bet. Quiet pockets of eddy water behind large boulders often produce fish.

Therein lies the secret of river walleye fishing — find 'em first and then catch them. If an angler has caught walleyes on a remote Canadian stream, they can do the same in the flowing waters of the Lower 48.

This isn't meant to be a how-to piece on fishing Canadian streams although the information is as sound for those waters as for the United States and its abundance of walleye rivers. Many states have rivers that produce superb walleye fishing. Michigan's Muskegon River is a good bet, and so too are the Detroit and St. Clair rivers near Motown. The Tittabawassee River flows into the Saginaw river and then into Saginaw Bay on Lake Huron at Bay City, and they are as different as night and day when compared to other state streams. Michigan's Kalamazoo River is another solid choice for walleye fishermen, and hotspots abound just upstream from Lake Michigan.

Photo by Paula Martin

Missouri River

But walleye fishing isn't limited solely to Michigan and its streams. The Missouri River, from Montana to North and South Dakota, offers truly spectacular angling. Washington's Columbia River is home to some truly huge walleyes; Wisconsin has its Fox River walleye run; Minnesota and Iowa has the Mississippi River, Ohio has the Ohio River, and the list could go on indefinitely.

Suffice it to say that river fishing is an excellent way to make the walleye connection. If walleyes are present, and even though the water is moving, the fish can be caught.

The trick to river fishing, as with lake fishing, is to know how and where to find fish. Lakes have various types of structure that hold fish, and rivers do as well.

River structure is different in one respect: moving water forces fish into certain areas at certain times. Finding fish in a river isn't brain surgery; it's more a matter of using common sense to dictate location.

River water means current, and breaks in the current are the primary places to try. The current and bottom or shoreline structure,

Mississippi River

act as a funnel for walleyes. These gamefish seldom fight heavy current flow but will home in on certain structure breaks to find comfort, food and safety. Everything a river walleye does hinges on current and structure.

These current breaks come in many forms — rock piles, bottom rubble, wingdams, shoreline points, underwater points or shelves, bridge abutments, docks, shoreline riprap, flats, submerged humps, boulders, logjams, merging currents, backwater eddys — all can and will provide the necessary comfort, food and safety requirements that walleyes need.

If you are not catching fish being quiet, kick the log jam to move the fish around. They won't leave, it just moves them around.

Walleyes, like salmon or

trout that periodically inhabit rivers, are comfort conscious. They prefer holding near structure that will break the current flow.

A river 'eye may hold in front of, behind, alongside or in any piece of structure that creates a current break. This break forms a pocket of quiet water, a cushion of quieter and more comfortable water that allows fish to pause, rest or dart out into the current flow to feed. These pockets of quieter water may be big or small, and larger pockets usually hold more gamefish.

I've learned a very important thing while fishing tournaments on major river systems. Water levels can change where walleyes hold, and a change can occur two or three times in one fishing day as rain or runoff raises the water level or when the water level recedes.

For instance: once, while fishing Michigan's Detroit River during the spring spawn as runoff swelled the river flow, the only place we could find catchable walleyes was near shore where high water flowed over riprap that normally was only six inches under water. The high dingy water conditions now meant that four feet of water covered the rocky area at the downstream end of a shoreline walkway.

The current was just too strong for walleyes in midstream. We tried those areas, and as we moved downstream past the walkway and its riprap, I pulled in near shore. There was enough current for a decent downstream vertical presentation, and we shortlined those fish. A quarter-ounce jig, tipped with a minnow, was bounced off bottom, and all the fish in that area of the river were concentrated on the lip of the riprap where it met bottom.

My first strike produced a dandy 8-pound female. My partner followed quickly with a similar sized fish, and we caught and released 10 fish to 11 pounds off that one tiny piece of structure.

Again, common sense combined with some walleye knowledge, dictated where to fish. No walleye would be fighting the full thrust of the current when it could find comfort and an available food supply in slower, shallower water with current breaks.

It's important for new anglers to focus in on key items when considering where, when and how to fish a river. The three key words — comfort, food, safety — should dictate how to choose a fishing location on any stream.

Anglers have long known that reading a lake is the key to success. It's no less important on a river, and learning to read running water is every bit as easy. In fact, I feel it's easier to read a river for probable walleye hotspots than to read a lake.

Walleyes, like salmon, trout or other gamefish, use the current to their advantage. They face upstream, take up a holding location, and allow the current and nearby structure to funnel food to them.

It is important for beginning walleye anglers to understand that although river walleyes hover and feed within a few inches of bottom, and face upstream, that upstream to a fish may mean the walleye may be facing sideways to the main flow. Look at the current, and especially where conflicting currents meet, and it's easy to understand why fish often are found facing sideways to the general downstream water flow.

Understand that single key point, and you'll have mastered an important part of reading current flow and determining where fish will hold near bottom.

Structure is important in a walleye's life. They rest near structure, feed near it and find safety near it. Structure to a river walleye is similar to the relationship between us and our kitchen, dining room, living room, bedroom and basement. The angler must understand this relationship between structure and the walleye's three important elements of comfort, food and safety.

What is structure? It can vary dramatically from one river to another. As I stated earlier, some rivers are deep while others are shallow. Some have fast currents while others do not. Some are sandy bottomed while others are rocky, and some are known as big-fish producers while others produce only smaller fish.

Each river has a character all its own. Some are in near-virgin wilderness areas while others flow within easy casting distance of millions of people. Regardless of the type of river, structure is the name of the river walleye fishing game.

Seasonal movements are an important part of any river fishing trip. Gamefish like walleyes are influenced by rising or lowering

water levels, barometric pressures, wind shifts, bright sun, spring runoff and hundreds of other factors.

I'm mindful of a spring trip several years ago. The spawn was underway, and we were fishing a wingdam on the Mississippi River. We began fishing directly in front of the wingdam but the water current was heavy — too heavy for spawning fish to hold there so we moved downstream and found a stretch of slower water.

We began checking out rockpiles, shoreline breaks or pieces of shoreline sticking out into the current, scattered pockets of rubble on bottom, and we soon found the fish. Instead of battling strong current, they had moved into an area with a slower current to spawn. Once we found the fish, a limit catch was soon made.

Weather and prevailing conditions are an important part of the river fisherman's repertoire. This knowledge allows savvy anglers to start thinking like a walleye, and putting themselves in the fish's place. Thinking comfort, food and safety would indicate an area out of the heavy current for spawning purposes. We found the area and we found the fish.

This is as good a time as any to mention feeding sprees. I, and countless other tournament anglers, have learned that there are aggressive and nonaggressive feeding times every day. If we could accurately predict when an aggressive bite would take place, we'd fish only at that time.

Seriously, the only surefire way to fish those peak periods when walleyes seem ravenous is to fish hard all day. We live for those really aggressive times when river walleyes go on the prowl and gobble everything in sight, but it doesn't happen nearly as often as we'd like. The key thing is to be on the water when they happen.

It also pays to be versatile and adept at several river fishing techniques. Much has been written in recent years about vertical jigging, and it's a dynamite technique. But, it isn't the only river fishing method I use.

As productive as vertical jigging is on most streams, there is a way to make this technique even better. Once, years ago, I watched a man jigging for yellow perch through the ice. He drilled two ice

 **97**

holes close together, and jigged a minnow-baited Russian spoon in each hole by using two rods. His success far surpassed any other angler on the ice that day.

That thought came to mind early in my tournament fishing career. If one rod is good, would two rods be better? I decided to give it a try, and the results were a genuine surprise. I immediately began hooking more walleyes, and the reason is simple.

Two rods with a jig on each line produces twice the opportunity to catch more fish. There is twice the glitter from lip-hooked minnows, twice the movement, and the technique provides twice the coverage area while bouncing jigs near bottom. This single fishing technique has delivered some excellent catches that may not have otherwise occurred.

The two-rod system requires practice to perfect. Once mastered, the results speak for themselves.

Several other river fishing techniques that anglers should try include casting lures; flipping jigs or crankbaits to key structure breaks; using jigging spoons; dragging a rig on bottom with a leech, minnow or nightcrawler; slow trolling a Rapala upstream on a 3-way rig; or working shoreline structure after dark (especially in late fall) with a cast or trolled crankbait. These specific techniques are included in other chapters.

Reading the river and the use of good electronics are important parts of an river fisherman's strategy. But there are tricks that anglers should know about river fishing that only good advice or experience can teach.

One is to recognize areas where river currents meet. Examples include where slower current meets faster water, or where side channels meet the main river channel. The area where two converging currents meet act as a collection point for walleyes. The fish find a cushion of quieter water alongside, in front of or behind these converging currents, and they don't have to move far to get their daily food supply. Even a slower current on the inside of river bends where it meets faster currents from the outside river bends will create slack water areas for feeding or resting fish.

Often, two current flows that meet can be seen by studying the surface. Such locations are revealed by debris floating on the surface in a continuous pattern that often forms a noticeable slick, and it doesn't take a wizard to spot them. Study river currents and you'll soon learn where these hotspots are found.

The area where a river current flows into or out of a lake can be a real hotspot. Fish often stage in such areas in the spring before the spawn or in the fall as they search for more food. Look for structure breaks on bottom at the inlet or outlet of a lake, and then puzzle out how to best fish each area.

Rubble, rockpiles and underwater humps are easy to find with a quality flasher or graph. I like underwater humps because they often hold fish, and if found in fairly shallow water (under eight feet), fish the dark side of the hump away from the sun on a bright day. Such humps also provide good nighttime sport.

Big-river walleyes often hold near bridge abutments. The pillars that hold the bridge up provide current breaks, and fish often hold along the sides or downstream from each abutment. Look for minor

structure breaks around the major break. For instance: the major structure break will be the abutment itself, and a minor break will be rock or rubble that collect on bottom. At times I've made some excellent catches along the upstream face of a bridge abutment, but more often than not, the sides or downstream end will be more productive.

Such breaks on structure are key locations to fish. Bridge abutments also attract walleyes on bright sunny days. The bridge will throw a shadow on the water, and this shadow will move

according to the sun's position. Learn about bridge abutments, and river walleyes will become much easier to catch.

Flats are another type of structure that walleyes favor, particularly in the spring after the spawn. Flat portions of the river, especially out of the main current flow, offer comfort and food for hungry walleyes. Fish often move onto the flats (they can be from five to 15 feet deep) to feed, and such areas often are ignored by other anglers.

Islands in a free-flowing river often produce good walleye fishing as well. An island is a major current break, and a rocky hump or shelving rocky shoreline along the river can be an excellent place to contact fish.

Backwater eddys and side channels off the main river channel can hold fish, and are often overlooked by river fishermen. Fish often hold on specific structure in the slow water, but they can hold at the edge of the current where it swirls into the eddy. Fish will hold near the current where it is easy to dart out for a quick meal, and these areas are easy to pinpoint. Floating debris often drifts into an eddy, and the first place to try is where the slow and faster currents meet.

Wingdams are key locations on big-water rivers. They were made by the Corps of Engineers by piling riprap from shore out to the middle of the river. The construction of wingdams force most of the current down the middle of the river in an attempt to prevent buildup of sediment that could restrict barge traffic.

The upstream side of wingdams offer the most predictable fishing action but don't ignore the tip or backside of the dam. Concentrate angling efforts on the tail-out or washout area of wingdams. Look for areas of heavy current flow through the wingdam because this will indicate where riprap has been knocked out, and this creates washouts that attract walleyes. Riprap along the wingdam will hold fish.

Remember that the upstream side of a wingdam will be the most productive location. Troll these areas with a 3-way swivel rig with live-bait or crankbait on a fairly short leader. The face of a wingdam isn't always good but more often then not it will provide some memorable fishing.

Deep holes will hold fish but it's been my experience that walleyes holding in such areas are commonly associated with bottom debris like rocks, boulders or remnant wood that has washed into the hole. The tailout portion of a hole often holds feeding fish, and try to key in on that area where the bottom starts to shelf up before spilling into the next riffle or stretch of fast water.

Channels are good, and one place where I've taken walleyes in the St. Clair River, which serves as the International Boundary between Michigan and Ontario, are the channel edges. This big, fast-flowing river is used by big ships, and the main channel is 20-30 feet deep. I've caught walleyes in the night and day time by anchoring next to the channel and hippety-hopping a jig up the channel wall. This can be very productive during summer months, and the biggest and best fish are caught after dark.

Rivers are a magnet for walleyes, and some of the best streams produce kingsize fish. Walleyes live in rivers year 'round, and that means good fishing for walleyes of several year classes. Big fish, small ones, and walleyes of medium size thrive in a river environment.

Learn to read a river, develop a sense of where fish should hold, and use common sense. The philosophy of a river providing comfort, food and safety is paramount to your success.

Combine these factors with the specialized angling techniques that are outlined in other chapters, and you'll be on your way to becoming a skilled fisherman.

Photo by Gary Roach

Tom Neustrom with his Rainey River (Minnesota) walleye.

Spring Ice Breakup

Spring

Spring is a time of renewal. Ice begins to loosen its grip on northern lakes, and as the weather warms, frost goes out of the ground and anglers eagerly await the walleye fishing season.

Hen walleyes, heavy with ripening ovaries, start moving toward lake reefs, shallow shoals or moving water. Some fish begin heading upstream toward spawning areas, and the rite of spring begins.

It's important for anglers to know that spring fish require different fishing presentations than during the summer or fall months. Cold water makes prespawn and spawning walleyes sluggish, and to cash in on this fabulous sport one must have a better than average knowledge of what angling techniques work and why they do.

This chapter is vitally important to four-season fishing action because walleyes caught during prespawn conditions are often the heaviest of the year. And, for those anglers who have been locked into a nasty winter in the upper Midwest, it's time to shake off the winter doldrums and head for open water.

In many states, ice-out coincides with the walleye opener. In other states, the season may be open year 'round. Whatever the case where you live, spring is a great time to catch a trophy walleye.

The fish usually are in a ravenous mood at this time of year, especially if you're lucky enough to have several days of stable weather before a fishing trip. After a long winter of cold water and lazy, slow motion feeding, a walleye's metabolism kicks into high gear. More food is available, and winter-weary fish are feeding.

It's prespawn now, and fish are preparing for the yearly spawning ritual. While the ice melts and the water warms, many walleyes will move from the lakes into the rivers. Others, in lakes without

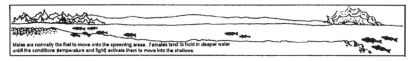

Males are normally the first to move onto the spawning areas. Females tend to hold in deeper water until the conditions (temperature and light) activate them to move into the shallows.

Courtesy of In-Fisherman

tributaries, will stage near shallow gravel or hard-bottomed areas. Males frequent these areas as they look for spawning females. Hens also will be cruising key areas as they await warming temperatures so they can spawn.

Photo by Roger E. Peterson

If an angler gets into one of these areas at the right time it's possible to find some fantastic action. Reservoirs are interesting waters to fish because of the variety of structure available. River walleyes were probably trapped when the dam was built, and have since adapted to reservoir habitat in different ways. As a result, the fish are scattered over several types of depth or bottom structure.

Start by following the old river bed toward its source and look for those fish that will spawn in the faster moving water in the reservoir's headwaters.

Before walleyes spawn, they stage in predictable locations. Look for fish to hold in deeper holes just below barrier areas that slow or halt their upstream migration.

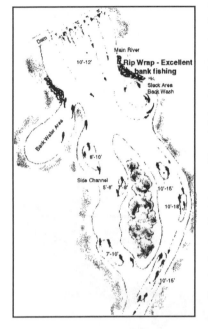

Water directly below a dam, and downstream for about five miles, are usually good bets for prespawn river fish. Other areas that can be productive include holes below long shallow stretches of river; slow water directly downstream from high current areas; and river bends below long straight stretches of the river.

Look for feeder creeks that run into the reservoir and the main river. Not all feeder creeks are alike. Those that flow through deep or shaded valleys will not warm as fast as those that run through wide-open walleyes.

Runoff from open valleys will receive more sun exposure and will warm faster. These feeder creeks usually warm first, so the earliest spawners will be in or around them.

Anglers also will find walleyes in the main reservoir in the shallow hard bottomed or gravel areas, and around riprap and in some weedy locations. Some fish prefer to spawn in reed beds. The key to early

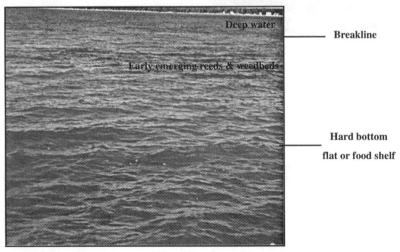

spring fishing success is to find a large flat or a food shelf of shallow water between one and eight feet deep.

It should be near deep water. Walleyes prefer having a place to hide nearby. Weather and water clarity has an effect on how shallow fish will be or even if they will be in the area. In clear or slightly stained water, a calm, sunny day will more likely chase fish into deeper water or the weeds.

If the water is stained, muddy or waves are breaking, even on a

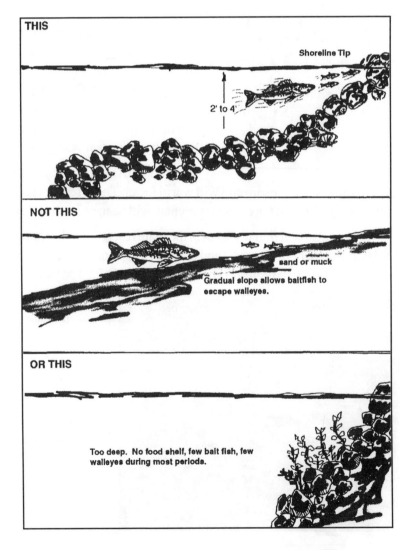

THIS

Shoreline Tip

2' to 4'

NOT THIS

sand or muck

Gradual slope allows baitfish to escape walleyes.

OR THIS

Too deep. No food shelf, few bait fish, few walleyes during most periods.

clear water lake, reservoir or river, light conditions will have little or no effect on how shallow walleyes will go or how long they will stay there. If there is a rocky shoreline, look for fast dropoffs next to shore or islands.

When fishing shallow water, it's very important to keep noise levels down. Walleyes are very sensitive to noise and vibration. Use an electric trolling motor to move through shallow water so fish won't be spooked.

Anglers must find walleyes before they can be caught. I prefer searching for schools of fish with an Eagle Graph. Once they are located, the best techniques include vertical jigging, trolling crankbaits or using bottom bouncers with spinners.

Vertical jigging comes first. At this time of year, the fish will be in the

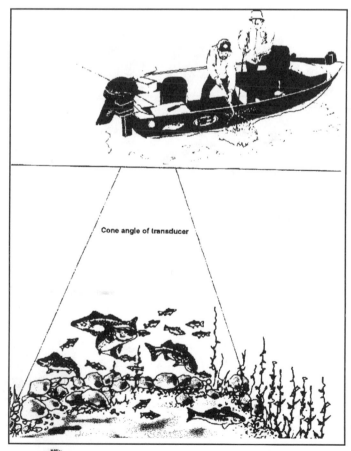

Cone angle of transducer

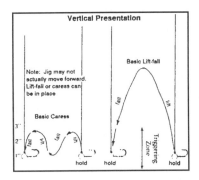

Courtesy of In-Fisherman

tributaries, in submerged river beds near the upper end or tight to shore on gravel or mud flats or in ripraps areas.

When fishing an area with some current, such as a feeder creek or the upper portion of a reservoir, vertical jig and slip along with the current to cover the most water in the shortest possible time.

Boat control is very important when vertical jigging. The trick is to move downstream at the same speed or slightly slower than the current. It's easy if there is some wind, but when a stiff breeze blows, any effect of the wind must be compensated for with an electric trolling motor.

Photo by Bob Jensen

I find that a bow-mounted, foot-controlled electric motor is best for boat control while vertical jigging. A foot control allows anglers to fish with two rods while positioning the boat, and in most situations, this results in more fish.

To control the boat, position it with the bow into the wind, and

use short power bursts from the electric motor to compensate for the wind. If this sound less complicated, it isn't.

One shortcut to river boat control is watch the line. A fishing line will tell you which way you must move the boat to keep the line and lure directly under the boat. If the line sweeps upstream, power the boat in that direction until the line is vertical again. A highly visible line like Trilene XT's Solar is a big help for this type of fishing because it is highly visible to the angler.

When casting, anglers can see those hits that are impossible to feel when using monofilament line. It's possible to catch more fish — especially the light strikers — if this type of line is used. Any line twitch could be a fish, but a hook-set must be quick to prevent the fish from dropping the jig.

Often, by the time an angler feels a hit, it's too late. Highly visible line can make a difference in very clear water, and when water clarity is like looking into a bottle of spring water, I will switch to a standard monofilament like Berkley clear XT.

Over the years I've used many different bow-mounted electric motors, and the one that is most user friendly, is the 36-volt Motor Guide. They are easy to use, but more importantly, they require little physical exertion when making turns or course adjustments.

Fishermen really appreciate this aspect after a long day on the water, and especially when vertical jigging or when fishing in strong wind. Models are available to handle any size of fishing boat.

Nightcrawlers work in the spring, but minnows are more effective. The best minnows will change from one river to another, and should be matched to the local forage base. In Michigan's Detroit River, a large river that separates Michigan from Ontario, it's tough to catch walleyes on anything but emerald shiners. On other rivers in western Michigan, fatheads or river chubs will out-produce shiners. Walleyes feed best on forage minnows they are accustomed to seeing.

In cold water, prespawn walleyes are not very aggressive. If the fish hit short, and strikes are missed, add a stinger hook to the jig-minnow rig.

Northland Fireball jig and minnow with stinger hook.

If there is little or no current in the reservoir, or the current is very slow, use the electric trolling motor to move the boat along over food shelves and dropoffs. Fish from the bow with a rod in each hand, and control the boat with the bow-mounted motor.

Photo by Dan Donarski

Hop and drag jigs along bottom or lightly lift and drop the lures you move along. Constantly adjust line length to match the depth. Slow fishing is more productive in cold weather because fish require more time to react to the bait-lure presentation.

When a good area is located, put out a marker buoy and work it thoroughly with jigs. Experiment with jig and minnow sizes, jig colors and jigging strokes.

One of my favorite jigs for early spring fishing include Northland's reliable Fireball or their Stand Up Fireball in chartreuse or orange with or without a stinger hook. If walleyes are sluggish, a stinger hook will help put more fish in the boat. Often, fish nip the minnow's tail and it's easy to miss them. A stinger hook gives a jig more zing.

Normark's bullet head Foxee Jig is excellent when casting and working jigs in the current. The head design is more streamlined, and this shape will allow anglers to get down deep with less drag.

Photo by Gary Roach

When fishing a stinger hook, the primary jig hook should be inserted through the minnow's mouth and out the top of the head. The stinger is then placed behind the dorsal fin. When rigged in this manner, short biting fish are no longer a problem.

Jig weights can vary from 1/8- to 3/8-oz., depending on the depth and the current speed. I usually tip a jig with a minnow or piece of crawler to add some flavor to the offering.

Adding plastic grub bodies like Berkley's Power Grub or Northland Screw-Tail to a jig or jig-minnow combination can be very effective. A grub body provides an action and scent to the rig, and this is especially true when Power Grubs are used.

The use of plastic grub bodies make it easy to experiment with different colors, and it also makes the overall offering look larger. It's always a good idea to use plastic bodies to help fish see the bait

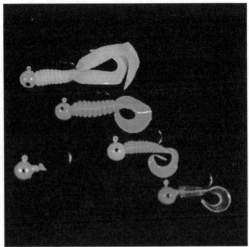

in stained or muddy water.

Plastic grub bodies do not work well with the compact Fire-Ball Jig. When using plastic, use a Northland Sink 'N Jig or Lip-Stick Jig or Blue Foxes Foxee Jig.

One trick for muddy water conditions is to add rattles to a jig-minnow combination. The best add-on rattles I've seen are the Buck-Shot Rattle Rings by Northland.

These rattles can be added to any jig head, spinner bait, jigging spoon or your favorite lure. Rattles can make anything work better under the proper conditions.

There really isn't a best way to work jigs for pre-spawning walleyes. Some days fish want a slow lift-and-fall technique, and other times they prefer a quick snap. It's best to experiment and determine which technique works best.

The tricky part is remembering what you did when a fish was hooked. Always be aware of how the jig was worked and at what depth produced a strike. Once a fisherman determine what works, stick with it.

Prespawn river walleyes usually are bottom huggers. It's usually best to work jigs no more than six inches off bottom. If a jig stroke lifts the jig-minnow a foot off bottom, at least half of your fishing time will be spent with the rig out of the strike zone.

One good way to locate fish is to troll minnow imitating crankbaits, like the No. 9-11 CountDown Rapala. They can be trolled up and down feeder creaks and along structure. In the spring, the best areas will have gravel bottoms or ripraps, but don't be afraid to troll tight to any brush sticking out from shore.

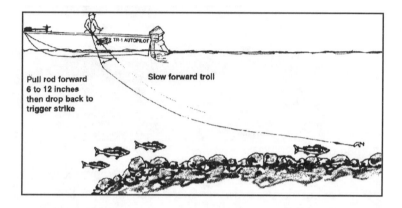

Once walleyes are located, mark the spot and work it thoroughly by casting cranks to the area.

Early in the year fish in natural lakes are often found relating to emerging weedbeds. Eel grass, cabbage and coontail are best, but any weeds can produce walleyes early in the growing season.

Forage fish in natural lakes and some reservoirs key on newly emerging weeds as their first line of defense against predation. With little in the way of natural cover during spring months, this new weed growth will get plenty of attention from baitfish that are looking to save their scales. Being the great opportunists that they are, walleyes key on these emerging

(L) My wife Paula and Eric working early emerging weeds with a Rapala for walleyes.

weeds for cover especially if baitfish are nearby.

The trick in the spring, as well as any other time of year, is to eliminate unproductive water and to spend time working water where the fish are. Right now, walleyes are constantly moving so finding catchable numbers of fish will require some work.

A rocky and gravel area in a back bay.

Look in the back bays where the water warms first. Walleyes like little patches of gravel and rock, especially in late spring if there is a late spawn. Anglers will find lots of male walleyes holding in these areas even after most of the females have finished spawning. Later, when the spawn has ended, it becomes a little tougher to locate fish.

Females move off into the muddy bottom structure areas and sulk. They're more likely to go for the easy meal so it's important to fish very slowly to give them time to respond.

Spring weedbeds aren't very thick so scout the lake for the thickest, early rising weedbeds and fish these areas with jigs or crankbaits. Walleyes also favor little strings of rock piles. If there are rocks and gravel that lead up into weed lines, that can be a big plus.

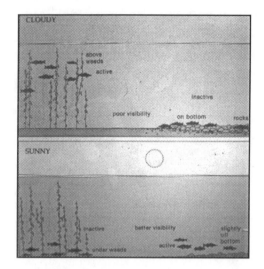

Courtesy of In-Fisherman

Weeds start growing in the shallows first and then will grow in deeper water as the season progresses. How deep weeds grow will depend on water clarity. Aquatic vegetation requires sunlight; in clear water lakes, weeds will grow deeper than in stained water lakes.

Water clarity can have an effect on when fish bite. An off-color lake may have a "daytime bite." A clear lake may have an "early morning or evening bite" because the fish hide in deep water structure and weeds during daylight hours.

Mud line coming out into the lake.

Fish around docks, pilings, newly emerging weeds, rocks, the

116

mud line or even a gravel or hard bottomed area in the middle of a muddy area.

Walleyes use weedy cover as an ambush point. Remember the relationship between cover and food is very important. Cover alone won't hold active, feeding walleyes unless there is food nearby.

Early in the year minnows move into the warmer shallows to spawn and walleyes follow them. If a cold front moves in, minnows will return to deep water and the walleyes will follow. It's a basic truism that walleyes are never far from their primary food source.

A few days of sunny weather and warm spring rain will activate leeches and insects in the shallows. Rain also will wash worms and nightcrawlers into the water. It's a savvy spring angler that has minnows, leeches and crawlers along when they go fishing.

Lipstick

Foxee

Photo by Gary Roach

I prefer tipping jigs with minnows, leeches or pieces of crawlers. I'll also use live bait rigs or crankbaits. It's important to learn which minnow (shiners, fat heads, red tails, creek chubs, dace, etc.) is best for each body of water being fished. A walleye's food preference can change quickly so it's wise to have a variety of lively bait available.

When casting or slow, long-

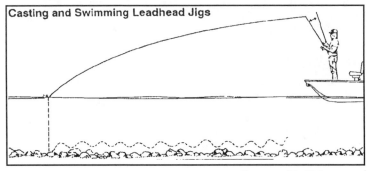

Casting and Swimming Leadhead Jigs

Courtesy of In-Fisherman

117

line trolling (also called snap jigging) in shallow areas, try a "stand up" jig head like Northland's Lipstick jig or Blue Fox's Slider Head jig. This type of jig head keeps the hook point up off the bottom so it's easier for the walleye to pick it up. Work the jig slowly; dragging, hopping and swimming it along bottom.

When casting, work these jigs all the way back to the boat. Let it sit for a second before picking it up to cast again. Give it a few jigs just in case a walleye is following it. That last twitch is often what catches the fish.

When snap jigging, move slowly along structure (water depth and weather conditions will dictate the jig weight to use) with an electric motor. Work jigs with a quick short snap of the rod every couple of seconds, and keep the jig at a little more than a 45-degree angle from the rod tip.

I've lately been using Blue Fox's new Stand-Up Foxee jig with Gary's new "Lip 'em & Clip 'em" stinger hook. The hook's "safety pin" clip can be inserted just under the skin of a leech, crawler or minnow, and it doesn't injure the bait as a barbed hook will do. It's probably the only stinger hook that will stay in a nightcrawler.

Whenever spring water is stained and the weather is windy, walleyes will move up inside the weedline and close to shore. That's when I will fan cast brightly colored (orange, chartreuse or hot pink) jigs or small crankbaits.

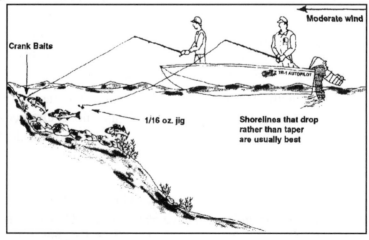

When fishing early-season weed edges, there are specific depths and locations that will usually produce. Find these precise areas, and perfect boat control can make the difference between catching a fish or two and taking a limit. For instance, if active fish are holding in 10 feet of water, and the boat is zigzagging between seven and 14 feet of water, it's probable that over half of your fishing time will be spent out of the strike zone. Fishing time is too valuable to spend half of it in nowhere land.

Subtle points and weed indentations also hold concentrations of early season walleyes.

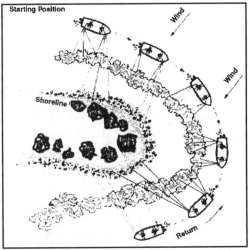

It's been my experience that if a few fish are caught and then they turn off, try experimenting with different colors to liven things up again. Another tip is to make sure the minnow on your jig is straight so it doesn't produce line twist. "Tune" your jig by hooking a minnow so it is in line with the jig head line tie.

If you fish with a friend, the use of the "split attack" method will produce more fish, faster even than when fishing alone. One person can work with jigs or rigs along a 10 to 12-foot dropoff while the other casts crankbaits to the weeds in 3-5 feet of water.

If you fish around emerging spring weeds, a No. 5 Shad Rap is a killer lure. Use a light rod like Berkley's Gary Roach six-foot-two inch medium action and you'll have plenty of fun. Choose a small reel like Abu Garcia's Ultra Light, load it with six-pound XT line, and it's possible to cast a crankbait a country mile.

I prefer silver over black Rapalas in clear water. If the water is stained, try a perch color or something bright like Normark's Fire Tiger color pattern.

Normark also has a shiny, silver metallic-blue color that is dynamite, especially for Great Lakes anglers who fish at night. Spring is a great time for night fishing because the fish are in the shallows where they are much easier to catch.

When walleyes get real finicky the best rig in your tacklebox is the Roach Rig, especially when a cold front forces fish into deeper, warmer water. The nice thing about this rig is you can slowly and methodically work an area with it.

Anglers can put a rig right on the fish and let the live bait do its job of enticing walleyes into striking. I use an air injected night crawler, plain minnow or leech with a Northland Gum Drop Floater or Blue Box Floatin' Foxee to keep it high enough so fish can see it.

Adjusting the snell on the rig to the right length is important, too. If you see fish three feet off bottom on your locator, use at least a 5- to 6-foot snell. You want the bait to be above the fish where it is more visible.

Structure fishing in water 10 feet or deeper with jigs and rigs demands that the line should never exceed a 45-degree angle from the boat. When a fish is seen on the sonar unit you know you're on target. When snap jigging, it's possible to have more line out which will create a greater angle.

I'm often trying to find fish on a new lake, and it's important to gather as much information as possible before starting to fish. It pays to talk to people who fish the area, and attempt to find out what works and what doesn't. Ask them when they caught the fish to learn if they were taken recently. Success stories from last summer are meaningless this spring.

Spring fishing requires a light touch, certainly lighter than during the summer when walleyes are more aggressive. Light tackle, small meals and slower movements are more effective than the more aggressive techniques used in July and August.

The key to spring walleye fishing is to be flexible and to experiment. Change jig size and color; try shallow and deep water; explore. Try using light line if you aren't getting action ... or slow down. Remember, it's possible to go too fast for walleyes.

One of the biggest mistakes novice anglers make when fishing live bait is they fish much too fast. Fishermen can't pull live meat through the water fast and expect it to interest many walleyes. It must look natural when fishing a floater or Roach Rig, and it must move a little and then remain motionless for a short period. When moving, water resistance will push bait near bottom. A brief pause will allow the bait to float up in the water column, and this often results in a strike.

The key to presenting live bait on rigs is to present it as naturally as possible. This is best accomplished through a slow methodical approach.

Fish as vertical as possible, and move the rig very slowly allow the bait to move and squirm on its own. Use a crawler, leech or minnow, and experiment by matching the tackle to the conditions.

In the spring, northern or Midwestern ground is saturated with water from snow melt and rain so runoff can cause muddy, high water conditions that challenge even the best walleye fisherman. Many

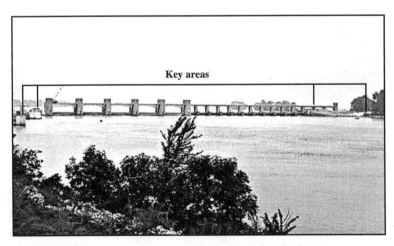

Lock and Dam areas are key spots to fish in the spring high water.

anglers panic when they look at bad water conditions.

The trick is to remember that the fish are still there. They must eat, and this means they can be caught.

If spring weather conditions deal a bad hand, just use your head and think what the fish would do and where they would go. Try to put yourself in the place of a walleye, and fish accordingly.

Spawning will take place anytime from late February through May, depending on where you live and the prevailing weather. Many walleyes will drop down rivers into a lake. The remaining fish will scatter widely from the tailwaters of natural falls and man-made dams to the lakes. On some large rivers with locks and dams, fish will disperse throughout the river system.

To make things tougher, during the spring, it's very common to encounter high water conditions. Never let high water keep you from the water; instead, take advantage of current conditions to find fish.

When the water is extremely high in rivers, walleyes will head for places most people wouldn't normally consider "walleye waters."

One of the most common mistakes people make is they tend to fish "memories." In other words, they'll use a technique that worked the last time they fished under normal water conditions when they had great success. That and they drift the middle of the river and expect to catch walleyes.

Photo by Jay Edwards

If water conditions have changed, walleyes will adapt to it, and anglers also must or they won't catch very many. When high water conditions occur, walleyes head for cover. They are not heavily-muscled fish like salmon or trout, and won't stay in the current when the water gets rough. They run for shelter from the current to conserve

This walleye was caught along the brush line in the river. (Notice the boat in background in the middle of the river he is "fishing memories.")

their energy and wait for food to come to them.

If the water goes over its banks, it is common to catch fish in places like flooded timber, off front lawns of river-front cottages, marinas or in backwater areas. Try to remember places you've seen during normal conditions with areas of ripraps, broken concrete, gravel or stone walkways. Walleyes will hold there in high water. Find areas of shelter, and it will be easy to find the fish.

Such locations will have some current and they will hold baitfish. A strong forage base will attract hungry walleyes.

123

Flooded rip rap and walkways.

Other excellent fish-holding places, often farther from the main river channel, are side channels, cuts, pockets, backwaters and adjoining lakes.

Certain places are hard to reach, and if you want to fish such places, you'll need to work into the rough stuff. Once there, drop or cast jigs along trees, pilings, logs and flooded timber. Try casting crankbaits, like a No. 7 Shad Rap or a Rattlin' Fat Rap, next to stumps and logs along shore. Often, the fish will only be a crank or two away from shore.

It's possible to cover a lot of territory by casting a crankbait, and it is an excellent way to locate fish fast. The next step would be to go back into these areas with a jig, and fish it slowly .

One important thing to bear in mind is that as soon as the water starts dropping, walleyes will quickly leave to avoid being trapped.

Follow them back to the river.

Even if the water is high, many walleyes will hold in the main river channels but will seek shelter along shoreline structure away from the main current. Hotspots are along wing dams near shore, and off points and islands that break the current flow. Try to remember where rock and gravel or riprap was in low water, and when high water covers it, go back and fish it. It can be a walleye magnet.

Holes and cuts that would normally be too shallow during regular water levels will now be prime spots. Especially if they are near shore and lined with gravel and rock.

Walleyes are sociable fish. They are famous for schooling together, and if you find a good area with even one walleye, chances are there are more nearby. Pockets of fish may be tough to find in high water, but when you do, fish catches can be fantastic.

Current break

A shoreline point causes a current break.

Culverts that drain water back to the river are always worth fishing.

As water conditions return to normal, a few fish may still be found in these backwater areas. However, they are usually small fish. Turn your attention back to the main river channel where larger fish will be found.

If the water is muddy, and visibility is measured by just a few inches, anglers must almost hit the walleye on the head before they will see, smell or hear a bait or lure. There are several jigs to try during high water that will do the job.

SOUND AND VIBRATION

Two jigs — the Northland Whistler has a small propeller that adds flash and vibration, and the Buck Shot Rattle by Northland with rattle chamber —will help fish zero in on the bait from a greater distance.

COLOR

Use bright colors like chartreuse, green, orange, hot pink, two-tone, etc., to increase jig visibility as much as possible.

There are two techniques that work in high water. One is "flipping" or tossing a jig into the heavy cover. Another is drifting and vertical jigging or "slipping" with the current.

Flipping is a technique that works for walleyes, panfish, bass, brook trout or any other fish that holds in small hard-to-fish areas. When flipping in high water, use an electric motor to control the boat in the current so you can hold near brush while a jig is worked in brushy pockets. My bow-mounted Motor Guide enables me to get into those small, tight areas and hold in the current without much effort. Make sure the electric motor has enough power for your boat to overcome the current.

Flipping requires patience. Work slowly and fish behind every tree, bush and rock. Any obstruction along shore is a potential fish-holding area. Work sea walls, docks and break areas as well.

A pattern will soon develop. Anglers may find that fish are holding behind, in or in front of the brush. If most of the hits come from the back side of an obstruction, concentrate fishing efforts in similar locations. At times, walleyes will be near brush but not in it.

They may consistently hold two feet from an obstruction in open water. That is a clue to fish around the brush from a distance, but don't forget to fish close to the brush as well. Keep moving and flipping.

It's exciting when you begin to connect with fish. You may approach a promising spot, and feel the adrenaline rush. Anglers can occasionally sense an upcoming good spot, and begin visualizing a

Photo by Paul Weikert

fish hiding there. But, make sure you fish all the spots that lead up to these areas.

Snags are a part of walleye fishing, and losing a few jigs is the price one pays to play this game, but a willingness to lose some jigs is what it takes to catch them in the brush. A good jig is Northland's weedless model called a Weed Weasel. It has a small plastic hook guard that should be softened up before use. Bend it up and down a few times to soften the guard so that when you get a hit, it's possible to get a good hook set.

If the river system has wing dams, walleyes tend to congregate along the full length. The best rigs for wingdam fishing are Northland Rock Runner bottom bouncers or a three-way swivel rig with a bell sinker and a three or four-foot snell rigged with a Floater or plain hook and bead or a Jig Rig. Sweeten it with a leech, crawler or minnow. Anglers also can shorten the snell length to two or three feet, and use a No. 3 Floating Rapala. Points and islands that break the current are good if there are rocks and gravel with deep water nearby.

An especially good combination to look for is a depression, hole or

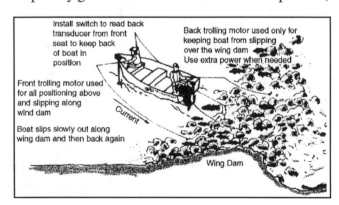

Install switch to read back transducer from front seat to keep back of boat in position

Back trolling motor used only for keeping boat from slipping over the wing dam Use extra power when needed

Front trolling motor used for all positioning above and slipping along wind dam

Current

Boat slips slowly out along wing dam and then back again

Wing Dam

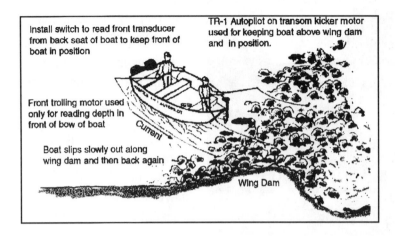

Install switch to read front transducer from back seat of boat to keep front of boat in position

TR-1 Autopilot on transom kicker motor used for keeping boat above wing dam and in position.

Front trolling motor used only for reading depth in front of bow of boat

Current

Boat slips slowly out along wing dam and then back again

Wing Dam

cut with a rocky, gravel bottom near a current break like an island or point. This combination offers walleyes a rich feeding and resting area.

Whenever I find a hole and start casting, an alternative to

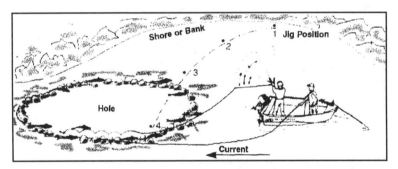

Shore or Bank

1 Jig Position

2

3

Hole

4

Current

anchoring is to use my Motor Guide Electric trolling motor to hold my boat in the current. Cast in front of the hole, and let the jig bounce down through the hole. Lift and drop the rodtip, and work the jig to the end of the hole before trying again. Each cast will be shorter and a little closer to the boat until the entire hole has been covered. Walleye will occasionally come up under the boat and use it as a current break. Work the jig

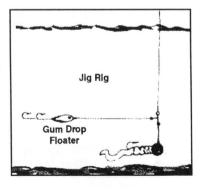

Jig Rig

Gum Drop Floater

vertically right along the edge of the boat.

My favorite jigs for slow to moderate current with an average depth of seven to 10 feet are Blue Fox's Bullethead and Northland's Fireball jigs in 1/16- to 1/4-ounce sizes. Carry a wide variety of jig colors and weights just in case it's necessary to experiment.

I recently began using a slick tackle bag. It's made by Plano and is called the "Tackle Logic System." It has separate, removable compartments and bags.

I can remove whichever compartment(s) I wish, and move it anywhere in the boat without having to move the whole bag or box.

One technique that works well is "slipping" with the current or vertical fishing. If you are fishing a bank line with two guys, one should flip into the brush while the other controls the boat and vertical fishes along the edges.

When slipping, it's important to keep the line as vertical as possible. Use an electric motor to control boat drift so it is moving at about the same speed as the current. Your fishing line can be used as an indicator; keep it as straight up and down as possible.

While slipping, "feel" the jig and constantly test for bottom. Walleyes will pick it up softly. If the line and jig is dragging, it will be snagging bottom and it will be difficult to tell if you've had a hit.

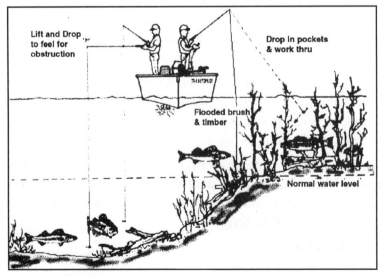

Remember, if you drag, you snag. There are a few tricks that can make a big difference.

Jig size: Use the lightest jig possible and still offer a vertical presentation. A walleye doesn't strike a jig, it inhales it. The lighter the jig, the easier it is to inhale and the more hookups you'll get.

Consider a fish's eyes. They are designed to look up and to each side. If you jig four to six inches off bottom, the jig is hitting them right on the nose. One reason to keep lifting and dropping the jig is to keep track of depth changes which allow anglers to adjust by letting out more line or reeling some in.

A tick or thump of a jig hitting bottom also helps get a walleye's attention. Never assume a jig is hung on bottom. Set the hook whenever a change of any type is felt.

Constantly test for bottom whenever drifting, and try to keep the bait just off bottom. Concentrate, and more often than not, you'll be ready for a strike when it comes.

If you slip slowly enough, your partner can flip to shoreline structure and fan cast the hole. Cast out, let it sink to bottom and use a slight lift-drop as it is worked back to the boat.

One suggestion for this type of fishing: buy some Berkley Solar XT or FireLine fluorescent green line. The visibility is excellent for daylight conditions. There are times when you can see a strike as the line moves before it can be felt. It's superior for vertical slipping because you can tell when it is up or downstream from the boat, and this will give anglers time to react with an electric motor.

I like to cast out and use a "pump & drag" retrieve with a pumping action while dragging the jig slowly across the bottom. As the rodtip is dropped to reel in slack line, watch the line carefully. If it jumps or twitches, set the hook. A big walleye probably has it.

One of my favorite rigs for fan casting is a Blue Fox stand-up jig or a Northland Whistler with a Screwtail or Power Grub. Try these jigs with or without live bait, and the 1/8 or 1/4-ounce sizes work best most of the time.

VIBRATION

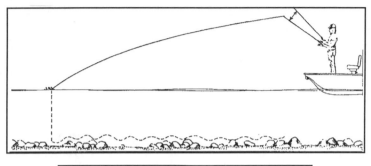

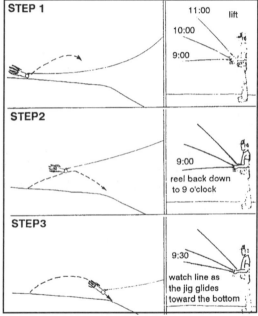

Courtesy of In-Fisherman

Pump and drag technique.

I mentioned the Whistler and the Buck Shot Rattler jigs, but even a round head jig like the Fireball or a Bullethead style like the Blue Fox Foxee jig gives off vibrations if you drop the jig. Lower the rodtip sharply and let the jig pound into the bottom. This causes a "thump" that fish can feel with their lateral lines. Walleyes will zero-in on a jig in muddy water and pick it up.

FIND THE PREFERRED DEPTH

Once I start catching fish, I pay close attention to how deep the water was where I caught my fish. I then use my Eagle graph to follow that particular depth throughout the river.

Walleyes have a preferred depth in a river. It depends on conditions, and most of them will be found in that general depth. If you drift aimlessly from shallow water to deep while slipping down the river, chances are good that a lot of productive water will be missed. Zero-in on the preferred depth.

In the spring of 1997, flood conditions were widespread throughout the Midwest, and water levels were 5 to 10-ft. above flood stage. The P.W.T. (In-Fisherman Professional Walleye Tournament) held their first event on the Mississippi River, and tree branches, muddy water and strong currents were everywhere we fished.

We fished locks and dams, backwater lakes, cuts and marinas, and caught a few walleyes in these slack water locations during practice runs. But as tournament day drew near, the river started dropping. This caused the fish to start moving out and back to the main river channel as the water receded. Many fishermen stayed in the backwaters, and the competition for fewer fish made for poor catches.

Randy Brandstra, an amateur contestant from Muskegon, Michigan, came along to fish the last day of pre-fishing practice with me. I decided to troll the main river since it might be the best bet with crankbaits. I figured it would be easier for a big fish to see a crank in the fast current and drifting debris. It was extremely hard to catch a walleye over 15 inches in such conditions.

I decided that using a Bellevue Rig, two Rapalas tied end to nose on the same line, might help catch some big fish. The Bellevue Rig was invented by an Iowa angler along the Mississippi River, and it has been a proven fish catcher. I used a five-ounce bell sinker, came up 1 1/2 feet to a 3-way swivel, and then attached a 2-foot piece of FireLine to the first Rapala. I then tied a 1 1/2-foot piece of FireLine to the back of the first Rapala and tied on a second Rapala.

Everything was tied on 20-lb. FireLine from the reel to the sinker.

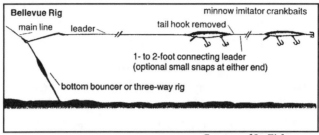

Courtesy of In-Fisherman

Twenty pound FireLine is the same diameter as 8-lb. monofilament, therefore it cuts the current and allows a more vertical presentation.

With FireLine you know when you hit bottom or know if you are dragging bottom. Since the Zebra mussel infestation, they can easily cut monofilament but FireLine is much more resistant to being cut by sharp mussel shells.

We began working the rigs upstream with the use of my 9.9 Mariner kicker and TR-1 auto pilot. This unit allows me to fish while it steers. I set my upstream speed slightly faster than a crawl and made adjustments with the hand held TR-1 remote control to stay in 10-12 foot depths. This depth was where most of the fish were being caught. I would lift and drop the 5-oz. bell sinker to bottom, making a thumping noise which would help attract fish.

We caught nice walleyes but lost quite a few. I wasn't happy with the missed hits or fish tearing off, and it caused me many hours of anguish before the tournament started. With water conditions as they were, three hits were all we could hope for. Many anglers never caught a single fish during the three-day tournament. We lost three fish during the first 30 minutes of the tournament before they could be netted.

I could see where they were hooked, and it dawned on me why they were being lost. They were hitting the first Rapala, and could not get their mouth around the lure. The line going back to the second lure kept getting in the way.

I remembered what a fellow competitor, J.R. Mazure, a pro fisherman from the Detroit, Michigan area, casually said at the meeting the night before. He said he was hand lining with two lures

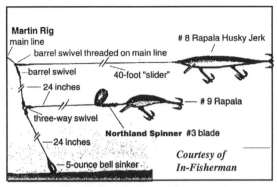

Martin Rig
main line
barrel swivel threaded on main line
barrel swivel
24 inches
three-way swivel
24 inches
5-ounce bell sinker
40-foot "slider"
8 Rapala Husky Jerk
9 Rapala
Northland Spinner #3 blade

Courtesy of
In-Fisherman

in the Detroit and St. Clair River Style. Bingo!

Within 15 minutes I invented the Martin Rig using a 5-ounce bell sinker, two feet up to a 3-way swivel which is attached to a two-foot leader and then to a Northland spinner on a six-inch leader. It was followed directly by a No. 9 floating Rapala two feet above the 3-way swivel.

I attached a Berkley Ball Bearing swivel to the main line before tieing it to the other end of the swivel, and then I slid on another ball bearing swivel on the main line so it will slide up but no further down than the 2-way swivel. To the slider swivel, attach a 40-foot length of FireLine; the length depends on the current and depth of water and the stick bait being used. It's important to vary the leader length so it is always just above bottom and doesn't get hung up. Personally, I like to use a No. 8 Rapala Husky Jerk crankbait.

After rigging up, we began catching fish within minutes. The spinner was a great attractant, and it helped keep the rig off bottom while helping to deflect floating debris. Once the trolling speed is set, lower the lure on the long leader into the water by hand before picking up the rod. Slowly ease other crankbait on the 3-way swivel and bell sinker over the side until it touches bottom. Maintain some contact with bottom with a lift and drop as the boat slowly trolls upstream with a The TR-1 auto pilot control in your hand to make slight speed direction, depth and current adjustments.

When fish are hooked, reel in and carefully check to see if it is hooked on the crankbait attached to the 3-way swivel. If it is, net the fish; if it isn't hooked on the 3-way swivel rig, carefully swing the whole works up toward the front of the boat, decrease forward speed on the trolling motor, and the TR-1 auto pilot will hold the boat in place. Then you must bring the line in hand-over-hand to net the fish.

Using the Martin Rig I came in second, 1.31 pounds under first place. Angler ingenuity and trying a new technique is what made it all possible.

The whole point is don't just do what worked last time. Don't fish "memories." Experiment and explore. Try these techniques if you haven't done so yet and have fun doing it.

Back trolling with TR-1.   *Photo by Jeff Wood*

Summer

Times change, and anglers must learn to adapt. Fishing has always been that way, and will probably never change.

For instance. Twenty years ago, if you had told some of North America's best walleye fishermen that it was possible to consistently tap a vein of walleye gold 10 feet down over 30 feet of water on certain waters, they would have probably died laughing.

Photo by Gary Roach

Jay Edwards and Mark Martin trolling for Saginaw Bay walleyes.

That was then and this is now. Anglers have learned to catch summer walleyes in the shallows and at great depths, and they do so consistently. It's no fluke, but as our walleye knowledge improves and our fishing techniques change for these grand gamefish, some new wrinkles evolve to meet various on-the-water challenges.

Fishing competitively has taught me many walleye lessons, especially for bigger fish. One of the most important aspects of being competitive in walleye tournament situations is to learn how to fish effectively. And one of the most important is to show your bait or lure to as many fish as possible.

Let's face it, if only 10 walleyes see your offering, the most fish you could possibly catch is 10. On the flip side, if you show your wares to 100 fish and only half decide to eat, you still catch 50 fish. Get the picture?

Photo by Roger E. Peterson

Walleyes relate to structure, and walleyes like hard-bottomed areas. A common statement is: "You can find structure without walleyes, but you never find walleyes without structure."

In many respects, that would be correct and true statement. But, there's more, and that is why anglers must understand these gamefish during the summer months..

Walleyes do relate to structure and do like hard-bottomed areas but walleyes pay more attention to food than they do to structure. If in doubt, read the preceding sentence again because it's a fundamental success step. It's one of the first walleye truths that I learned and it is important.

The old saying would be far more accurate today if it had said: "You can find walleye food without walleyes, but you'll never find walleyes without food."

Anglers of the 1990's and the upcoming millennium have learned

that except for the spawning period, the location of walleyes is more often dictated by food availability than anything else. If there is plenty of food present, an angler can bet his favorite box of jigs there are probably walleyes around. Sure, they love structure, but only if food is available on it.

Conversely, in waters like the Great Lakes where an abundance of suspended forage like alewives and gizzard shad are found, walleyes will hang out and feed where the food is.

Photo by Roger E. Peterson

And that, my friends, means fish suspended over open water.

Ask anyone who spends time on Lake Erie, Saginaw Bay, Little Bay de Noc, Lake Winnebago or Lake Oahe where they find fish. They may say near weedbed edges, breaklines and reefs, but without a doubt they also will mention open-water suspended fish.

Trolling is the dominate fishing method when targeting open-water and suspended walleyes. Trolling allows anglers to cover more water, and if you use side planers, it's possible to cover plenty of water each day.

In-line planers work well in almost any walleye trolling situation where we want to increase the horizontal and vertical spread of trolling lines. Fish that are scattered across large flats or are suspended over open water, are good bets for in-line planer board presentations.

Photo by Gary Roach

The key thing to remember when trolling with the wind is that planer boards or in-line planers will help keep your lures evenly spread.

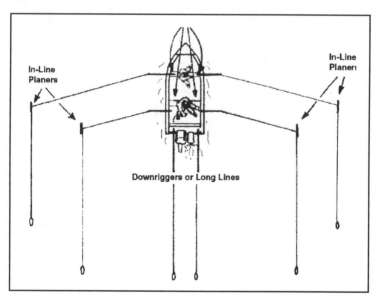

With-the-wind trolling speeds are more even, and there is another plus factor. When fish are hooked, anglers won't have to worry about the wind whipping the boat around and tangling fishing lines if you don't have autopilot.

When it comes to open-water walleyes, the more water an angler

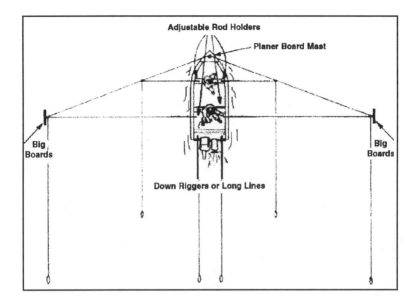

can cover, the more fish will see their baits or lures. It adds up to a heavier fish catch..

Open-water walleyes that suspend are nomadic by nature. When they are schooled up, they follow forage fish like a mule follows the proverbial carrot on a stick. Finding suspended walleyes means covering more water and using sonar to help find the fish.

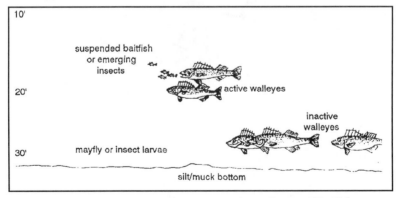

Courtesy of In-Fisherman

I've often spent a half-day just covering the water and watching my Eagle graph for baitfish schools or big schools of baitfish with big dark hooks nearby. Suspended walleyes are the easiest fish of all to spot on a graph.

If big hooks aren't being marked on the graph, don't waste time fishing that area. The one exception is when fish are suspended high in the water column.

If walleyes suspend in the top 10 feet of water, it's possible these fish may not be marked by a sonar unit. That's the bad news.

The good news is that when walleyes do suspend this high, they are usually very active feeders. This water can be eliminated quickly by pulling a spread of lures from the surface down to 10 feet. If a fish isn't caught in 10 to 15 minutes, fishermen can assume they are not there.

Once fish are found, try to stay on them. The easiest way is with a global positioning system (GPS). My Eagle GPS system is so simple that I figured it out without having to read the instructions. These units actually tell anglers what they must do, and basic use requires less than 15 minutes to learn.

Crankbaits are very popular for targeting open-water walleyes because they work. But, unlike humans, all crankbaits are not created equal. What works one day may not produce the next. I let the fish tell me what will be hot, and four factors must be considered:

Dave Dulaney attaching FireLine onto inline planer board.

Dave slowly letting presentation out with inline planer board to the desired distance off each side of the boat.

Randy Bandstra quick releasing inline planer board.

Randy helps Dave land a nice walleye.

Lure Action — Are walleyes responding better to lures with a wide wobble, or do they prefer them with a tight shimmy?

Lure Profile — Are the fish hitting wide body baits like a Shad Rap or Rattlin' Fat Rap, or do they favor long, slender lures like a floating Rapala?

Lure Size — Are the fish hitting big lures or small lures? Am I taking more big fish on large lures?

Lure Color — What colors are the most productive? It's important to note that color preference can quickly change.

Once I determine the best lure action, profile, size and color, I run that lure on every line, but may experiment a little just to keep the fish honest.

When it comes to trolling crankbaits for suspended walleyes, the most important thing is lure depth. If you mark fish 15 feet down, and the lures are running at 20 feet, it won't be a productive day.

Walleye respond best to baits or lures on their level or up just a bit. We used to experiment with different lengths of line-out to find the right depth. This trail-and-error method worked, but it ate up valuable fishing time.

There now is a shortcut to hitting the right depth with trolled crankbaits. I've been using Crankbaits "In-Depth" as a valuable trolling tool. This book was developed by Dr. Steven Holt, Tom Irwin and Mark Romanack, and it belongs in every fishing boat.

One of my secrets is to use 10-pound Trilene XT or 20-pound Fire Line. If anglers use these lines, the book will tell exactly how deep various lures will run with varying lengths of line.

Big schools of suspended walleyes like those found on Lake Erie, Saginaw Bay and other large bodies of water, are usually suckers for crankbaits trolled behind in-line planers. The key to this type of fishing is finding the most productive depth.

Suspended open-water walleyes are easy fish to see on a sonar unit. If it isn't marking fish, and if they are not suspended high in the water column, they are not there. Let's say big clouds of baitfish are noted 15 feet down with some big eyebrow-shaped hooks just below them at 17 feet.

I study my Eagle graph In situations like this, and target the bottom edge of the baitfish and fish just above the walleye's heads. In this particular scenario, that means lures should be trolled at the 16-foot level..

A favorite open-water crankbait is the Down Deep Rattlin' Fat Rap in the 7/16 and 5/8 oz. sizes. I know a 7/16 Rap runs 16 feet deep with 62 feet of 10 lb. Trilene XT, so I let out 62 feet of line from my Abu Garcia level-wind reel, hook the line to a Mr. Walleye Trolling board and send it off to the side.

This is just the beginning. The next step is to repeat this process with other lines using different colors and profiles, and different sized lures. When one bait starts to produce fish, I replace the others with the lure that is working. It all boils down to putting together a solid trolling pattern.

The number of people in my boat will dictate how many lines I can run. In Michigan, we can fish two lines per person. The more lines, and the more water that can be covered horizontally and vertically, the more opportunities a fisherman has to present lures to more fish.

With in-line boards, anglers are limited to two boards (lines) per side without having problems. If additional lines are needed, one or two flat lines can be run from the boat. The boat is the tool being used to push walleyes out to the side, so don't put the boards too far out. Forty feet for the furthest boards is a good distance, and then experiment with the inside boards. I run them as close as 10 feet off the sides and at other times 20 feet seems to be the magic distance. Fish don't charge off but will move out from under the boat and into the planer board lines.

Landing fish with a Mr. Walleye Board is quick and easy. While boards can be rigged to slide down the line on a strike, I find it works better to set the release tight so it doesn't release. Watch the bright orange boards like a bobber, and when it jerks back, jiggles or moves back out of formation there could be a fish on the line.

A big fish will actually pull the board behind the boat or under water. A hook set isn't needed because the fish will hook themselves. Once a walleye is hooked, pick up the rod and reel the board slowly to the boat. Maintain some tension on the board line, reach out and grab the board and release it from the line. The fish can now be fought to the boat on a weight-free line.

While cranks are usually dynamite on suspended walleyes, some days it takes meat to trip their trigger. At times like this, target these suspended fish with a spinner/crawler combination off a bottom bouncer or 3-way swivel rig. The new Gary Roach Super Clip Drop Weight system often makes willing biters out of non-feeding walleyes.

Super Clip Drop Weights feature the same clip release found on the Mr. Walleye planer board, and they come in a variety of colors. By varying the amount of weight on the bottom bouncer rigs or Super Clips, anglers can cover different depths of water.

If I mark fish high, only 10-15 feet down, I start with weights of 3/4-1 oz., and troll at 1.4-1.8 miles per hour. I let our 18 feet of line past the weight and clip it to the board, and this allows the spinner to run 12-15 feet deep, depending on the trolling speed.

It's important to pay close attention to the trolling speed when the fish are high in the water column and when using weights. If trolling speed increases, bait or lure will rise up and run shallower; slowing down will cause it to slow down and sink deeper.

I always keep one eye on the speed over ground display and the other on my fish finder when using weights, and this depends on where the fish are in the water column. I can speed up and cause my spinner rig to rise or slow down and cause the spinner to sink when fish are 20 feet or deeper.

Photo by Dave Dulaney
Walleye caught using the pendulum method.

Fish 20 feet or so will still be within your reach by taking the boat out of gear and letting the presentation pendulum down almost coming to a halt with the boards. Kick the motor into gear will cause the spinner rig to pendulum up as the spinners returns to the 12- to 15-foot depths. By using the pendulum method and watching your graph you can target many different levels of fish in the water column.

In July of 1993, my fishing and business partner, Gary Roach, won first place and $20,000 while I took second place and won $12,000 in the second In-Fisherman/Cabela's Tournament on Mille Lacs Lake, Minnesota. One of the keys that unlocked our success during that tournament was a very common rig that is named after the old master. It's the "Roach Rig."

Jigs and rigs are the most common and some of the oldest methods of catching walleyes. The definition of a rig is misunderstood by many beginning walleye fishermen. It's easy though; if you fish with a hook and splitshot, you're riggin'. If you push the splitshot down so it's touches the hook, you're jiggin'.

It does get a bit more complicated from there. The tackle industry has a huge variety of rigs and jigs to choose from, and many are designed for special situations and conditions. Each one is a different tool for a different job.

Through any fishing year, professional and amateur anglers will catch millions of walleyes with this endless variety of rigs. One of my obvious favorites, and certainly the most versatile and easily altered rig, is Northland's Roach Rig. Roach Rigs are made up of a quick-change "foot shaped sinker," a bobber stop and bead stop which allow fishermen to adjust the leader length. This rig also has a swivel, a leader (anywhere from 24 inches to 10-12 feet long) and a hook which can be a plain hook and bead or a floater like the Gum Drop Floater or the Floating Foxee.

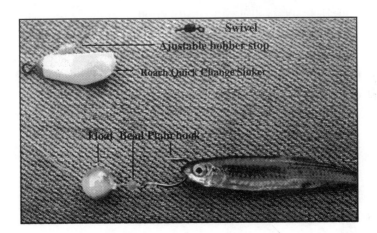

Our success during this particular tournament was the result of properly using a Roach Rig. Gary and I used identical rigs, as did our amateur fishing partners during the three-day event.

We were fishing a very large mud flat, and active fish were located on the edge of the flat between 27 and 31 feet of water. Nasty weather and heavy waves forced us to use special boat handling techniques to control our position and presentation. Two to four-foot waves tossed

Attaching a sea anchor to a bow cleat.   *Photo by Jeff Wood*

the bow of my boat up and down like a bucking bronco.

I filled my bow live well with water, plugged the outlet holes and let water overflow into the bilge to add ballast to solve the problem. It helped but it still wasn't enough to give adequate boat control.

So I attached a sea anchor tightly to the bow. This acted like a big fist gripping the water; when a wave tried to throw the boat up, the sea anchor pulled it down. The bow slowly rose only a few inches with a big wave instead of jumping several feet.

Now that my up-and-down movement was under control, I needed forward and reverse control. The big 50-pound thrust Motor Guide electric provided all the control I needed. This technique is one that only a pro or a very experienced boater should try. I wouldn't even attempt it with any boat other than my high sided, well constructed Lund Tournament Pro-V.

The walleyes were grouped in pockets along the edge. The "meal of the day" was a big, black and very lively leech. By using a 10-12 foot long leader on my Roach Rig, and a very thin, lightweight Tru-Turn hook with small red bead in front, we gave the leech the freedom to swim up, down and around.

We moved very slowly or remained motionless while fishing a

Roach Sinker ———————

Photo by Mark Romanack
My daughter Rachael and I with a walleye
caught using a Roach Rig.

spot. By holding the Roach Rig sinker six inches to 3-4 feet off bottom, and letting the leech's lively action antagonize the walleyes, we could cover from 6 inches to about three or four feet off bottom where the fish were located.

To keep our long leaders from tangling with each other, I sat in the bow of my Lund while my partner worked the back. I controlled the path of the boat very tightly with slow, continuous bursts of thrust from the electric motor so it would barely move along the dropoff edge.

My presentation was on the deep side while my partner worked the shallow side. If the walleyes were shallow or deep, one of us would catch a fish.

If conditions had been different, and had the fish been holding tightly on bottom, I would have shortened the leader so the leech was under tighter control and closer to bottom. Doing so is as easy as sliding the rubber bobber stop up or down the line.

Rigs work great under many different conditions, and not just on a mud flat edge. Fishermen can work rock piles (I won the first *In-Fisherman Cabela's* championship on a reef using a Roach Rig in 1990).

I've fished all over the United States and Canada, and rigging is always a reliable technique. Rigs let live bait do what they are supposed to do ... move. Anglers can control the bait, and its depth and position but live bait has the freedom to move and swim and attract hungry walleyes.

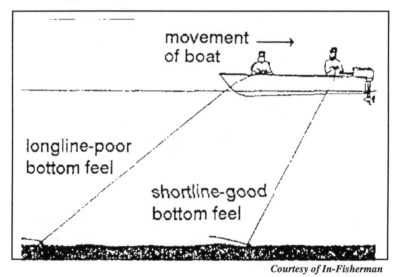

Courtesy of In-Fisherman

Rigs work in any lake or reservoir and on just about any type of structure. A good walleye stick can even work them in a river.

A couple important tips about rig fishing: Keep the line angle at no more greater than 45 degrees. In other words, keep the rig below your boat or as close to the boat as possible, and letting the rig down to bottom slowly so that your snell doesn't tangle back up with your main line. Put your bait in the water followed by the sinker. Then let it down 2 to 3 feet, and stop. Repeat until the sinker reaches bottom. You will then know your presentation is laid out without tangles.

I've had partners who plunked it over the side of the boat and let it plunge to the bottom. Twenty minutes later reel up to check the bait and have a tangled mess.

One feature that helps do this is a quick change sinker. If the current, wind or water conditions make it difficult to keep the rig close, the trick is to use a heavier sinker. With a soft wire eye on the Roach sinker, anglers can twist the eye open and replace it with a heavier weight.

One reason to fish near the boat is so the rig actually fishes the structure, and any nearby fish, that anglers see on their graph.

I use a state-of-the-art Eagle graph and an Eagle GPS unit that lets me lock fish-holding areas in a computer memory bank where they can be called up whenever needed. In the case of the Mille Lacs tournament, I found several good holding spots during pre-fishing and entered "way points" into the graph's computer for future reference.

A trick to remembering way points is to think of them as ways to get back to a good fishing spot. Fishermen can write down longitude and latitude numbers of specific way points in a notebook with specific information so that they can find them when needed.

The Eagle GPS also lets anglers mark "icons" or symbols near each way point. For example, I put a small fish icon to mark areas near way points where I catch fish. By recalling the way point on the screen later, I can see each way point and each nearby icon where I've caught fish.

My recorded information was invaluable in this particular tournament. As long as I was the first fisherman on those spots that day, I almost always caught fish. Whatever structure was down there would hold fish, and if it hadn't moved, neither would the fish.

This technology saves many hours of valuable fishing time. Once my way points and icons are marked as hotspots, I don't waste time fishing the unproductive water between them. I run from one spot to the next, and fish where the fish are.

This is a good combination. Combining old, proven tackle with new, high tech electronics can be the difference between success and failure in a walleye tournament. It's still tough fishing when the wind blows 30 miles per hour and waves are 4-5 feet high, but that's walleye weather.

An angler would be nuts to throw a crankbait into the thickest weeds, right? Not really. If that's where the fish are, that's where we must go to catch them.

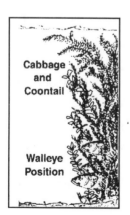

Some of the most overlooked walleye hotspots are in the weeds. Bass fishermen are experts at working the weeds; walleye fishermen can do the same. I've often heard anglers complain about catching walleyes during a bass tournament.

That should be an angler's first clue about potential summer hotspots. People who worry about hanging up all the time may be missing out on some of midsummer's best action.

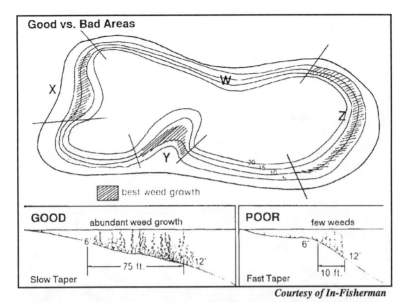

Good vs. Bad Areas

X

W

Z

Y

20
15
10
5

▧ best weed growth

GOOD	abundant weed growth

6'   12'
├── 75 ft. ──┤
Slow Taper

POOR	few weeds

6'   12'
├─ 10 ft. ─┤
Fast Taper

Courtesy of In-Fisherman

Many people have learned to fish structure and weedbed edges for walleyes, but few have considered fishing the thickest weeds. This can produce superb walleye action if the proper techniques are used.

Walleyes love thick, nasty weeds. They provide cover from bigger predators and sunlight, and best of all, weeds offer easy pickin's on baitfish.

Hey, prove it to yourself. Check a weedbed sometime with Polaroid sunglasses, and see how many small fish hide there. Where there's food, there's walleyes. Weedbeds are not automatically good; walleyes must have deep water nearby. Deep water can be a man-made channel, an old river bed or just a dropoff leading from the weeds into the depths.

There are many ways to make the best of a weedy situation. Try starting early in the morning by trolling wedbed edges with crankbaits or crawler harness. Some active fish may still be roaming the edges before disappearing into thick weed cover later that morning.

After trolling the outside, start working holes inside the weeds. Holes can be any opening from coffee cup-size to something as large as your boat. A strong, electric motor will move a boat through

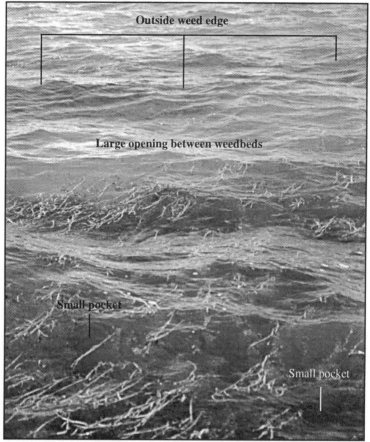

the salad. I use my bow-mounted 36-volt Motor Guide to move my Lund through the weeds.

Experiment with a variety of weed fishing techniques in low-growing weeds. Cast a shallow running No. 5 or 7 Shad Rap across the tops of the holes. The strikes are hard, and there is no problem detecting a hit.

In large open pockets, cast a Shad Rap or Husky Suspending Jerk at the far end of the pocket and work it back with a slight pumping motion. Once the lure hits the edge of the hole, lift it out and cast again. If a lure hangs in the weeds during a retrieve, give a sharp jerk to rip the weeds free. A brief hangup in the weeds often triggers a walleye strike.

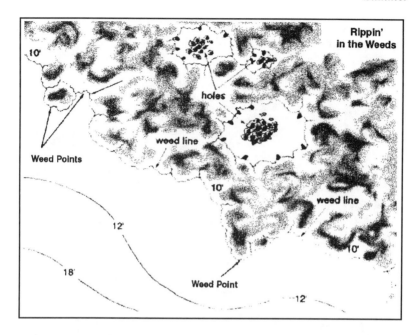

Try using jigs to work large weedy pockets. Blue Fox makes a dandy little Foxee Jig with a Slider Head that skims through the weeds. The jig eye is on the nose so the line will pull it through without getting hung up as often as with other jigs.

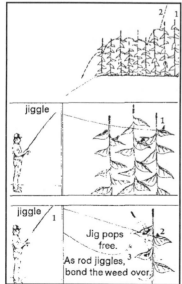

Courtesy of In-Fisherman

Another jig that works great in large weedy pockets is Northland's Whistler jig. The flash and vibration of its tiny propeller gets the attention of weed-bound walleyes.

Cast the jig into the hole and work it back slowly with a pumping action so that it rises and falls through the weeds and off the bottom. Watch the line for any indication of a strike, especially on the fall or when it sits on bottom. Berkley's bright green Solar XT

157

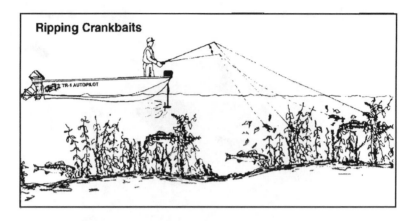

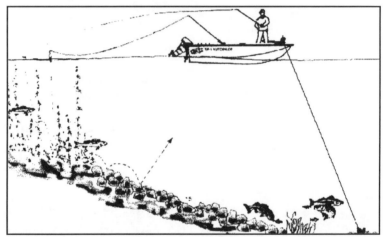

line is helpful, and I use it as a bobber. When the line twitches, set the hook.

When weedbed holes are small, try flippin jigs. Different equipment is needed for this technique to work. A long, powerful rod is important, and Berkley's 8 to 8 1/2-foot Salmon/Steelhead rod is perfect. It has enough backbone to pull walleyes out of the weeds, and it has the length needed to flip baits into pockets near the boat. It will allow anglers to cover more water before it's necessary to move the boat.

As far as reels are concerned, the most important elements are a smooth drag and a fast on/off anti-reverse switch. My Abu/Garcia

Photo by Jeff Wood

You will find walleyes on the outside edge and inside pockets of cane weeds.

open-faced spinning reel has a smooth, even drag and more ball bearings than most reels, and it has never failed me.

When I fish heavy weeds, I tighten the drag a bit more than normal, and let the long rod absorb shock when it's necessary to put pressure on a large fish. When needed, I can quickly flip the anti-reverse off and back reel.

I load my reels with Berkley 10-pound XT or 20-pound Berkley Fire Line. Both offer strength and resistance to abrasion, and that allows me to horse fish out before they get wrapped in the weeds.

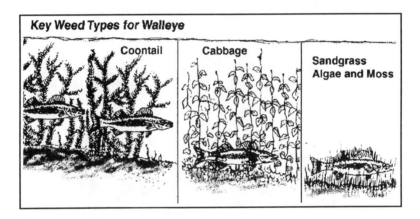

A few of my favorite flippin' jigs are Northland's Fireball or Blue Fox's Bullet Head. Use nothing larger than a 1/16th or 1/8th-oz. jig. Light jigs give better action as you bounce it up and down through a weedy pocket. Heavier jigs sink too fast for fish to react, and it's impossible to give them that enticing little wiggle that is

Pencil reeds will also hold walleye especially if there are rocks or lower weeds mixed in.

possible with a lighter jig. Tip the jig with a leech, small crawler, half of a nightcrawler or a minnow to add some flavor.

Move the boat into the weeds quietly, and flip or lower the jig into weedy holes or pockets. Lower the jig slowly, wiggling it as it falls to bottom. Pound it on the bottom , and let it sit for a few seconds. Raise and wiggle it to the surface.

As you work the jig, look ahead or around the boat for the next hole. When the jig hits the surface, swing it into another hole and try again. Don't waste time; work each pocket quickly. A fish may hit

HOT SPOT

in the first hole, but it's more likely to take 50 to 100 holes before the first fish hit. I never said this was going to be easy.

Reaction times for walleyes can be short in the tiny weed pockets, and jolting strikes are common. Fish often hook themselves..

Be careful while lowering the jig, and watch the line closely. Walleyes occasionally swim out and grab the jig. The line may twitch slightly or stop going down. If a fish is on, set the hook and get them to the surface quickly. The more a fish wrestles in the weeds, the lesser the chances are of landing it.

Walleyes are not evenly distributed throughout the weeds. They relate to structure inside the weeds. This structure may be as small as a kitchen table or as large as a house. Key areas to look for are hard gravel or rocky bottomed areas inside a weedbed, or any combination of two weed types. Another hotspot can be where mud meets a sandy bottom.

If success comes from one of these weedy hotspots, it's important to be able to find it again. If it produces fish today, chances are they

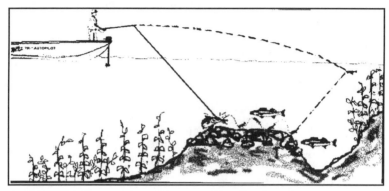

A good GPS helps you return to key spots time after time.

will be there on future trips.

This is where a GPS until will pay for itself. When a fish is caught, take time to punch in the coordinates and note the spot. It makes it much easier to find that hotspot again.

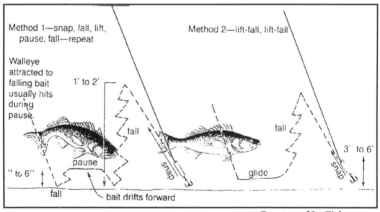

Courtesy of In-Fisherman

Any body of water that connects to the Great Lakes will produce huge schools of gizzard shad that are two to three inches long. They are a favorite food for foraging walleyes.

If a school of shad is found near a weedbed, walleyes will make feeding forays out of the weeds. Once they have fed they go back into the weeds. This can be a hotspot for aggressive, feeding fish.

Use a controlled drift on a windy day to work weedbed edges, and vertically jig a spoon like Northland's Fire Eye Minnow, Blue Foxes' Tingler Spoon, Hopkins' Spoon or a Crippled Herring. If there is no wind, use the electric motor to slowly work the weedy edges.

I call this "power snapping." Sharply raise and lower the spoon as you move along. Touch bottom, snap the wrist upward so the lure jumps straight up 1-3 feet, and then drop it back down. Use this action repeatedly, and fish usually hit on the fall or as the line is tightened during a pause.

I often use another technique called "rippin'," and it can turn a passive walleye into an aggressive fish. Throw a jigging spoon up into the weeds and let it settle along the edge or in a weedy pocket. Give it a good jerk back toward the boat, let it settle again and reel in slack line. When it hooks on the weeds, give a solid jerk. This can trigger walleyes to hit, and it also will blow weeds off the spoon.

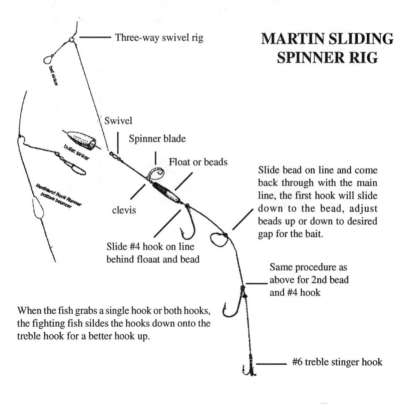

Three-way swivel rig

MARTIN SLIDING SPINNER RIG

Swivel

Spinner blade

Float or beads

clevis

Slide #4 hook on line behind floaat and bead

Slide bead on line and come back through with the main line, the first hook will slide down to the bead, adjust beads up or down to desired gap for the bait.

Same procedure as above for 2nd bead and #4 hook

When the fish grabs a single hook or both hooks, the fighting fish sildes the hooks down onto the treble hook for a better hook up.

#6 treble stinger hook

163

Gary Roach was fishing deep along a breakline and caught this walleye using a Shad Rap lure and lead core line.

Fall

Fall is truly my favorite time of year. Partly because of deer and grouse hunting seasons, but mostly because of some tremendous walleye fishing that is available until freeze-up. These fish are fattening up for winter, and they aren't heavily pressured by anglers. And, it seems they grow heavier with eggs with each passing day.

A 29-inch post-spawn spring walleye will weigh eight to nine pounds. That fish in November will weigh 10 to 11 pounds. And if that isn't enough, the cooling air and water temperatures seem to put more scrap in their fight.

Fall is a big-fish time. This annual feeding spree will plump them up, and they are much easier to catch than at other times of the year. Fall is definitely the key time to catch some of the year's largest

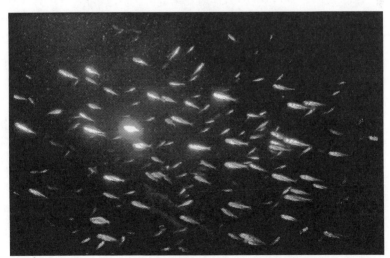

School of bait fish.   *Photo by Roger E. Peterson*

 **165**

walleyes.

Lakes and many rivers are filled with young-of-the-year gamefish that range from bluegills to bass. Schools of alewives, shad and other baitfish offer a buffet table of tasty eating for hungry walleyes.

Anglers willing to dress for the cold, frigid temperatures can have a good shot at catching a trophy fish, but it can be nasty. In northern lakes ice may be forming along lake edges and in quiet river stretches, and snow or frosty mornings are on tap.

Many anglers have hung up their rods, have winterized their boat and motor, and many people are counting the days until freeze-up and ice fishing begins.

But if you are a hardcore walleye fisherman, it's important to gut it out in hopes of catching a trophy 'eye. Fall fishing isn't as rugged as it once was. Today's miracle-age clothing is much better than the old-fashioned clothes we once wore. The important thing when dressing for cold weather is to dress in layers with cushions of warm air between the layers. Thinsulate or Gore-Tex clothing wick away perspiration, and any clothing that breaks the wind chill will keep you warm and dry. Chemical hand warmers will keep hands and toes warm.

A personal flotation device (PFD) can save your life if you fall overboard, but equally important, it also will help keep you warm as well.

Fall weather will bring walleyes up rivers just like spawning salmon. In September and October, they begin migrating after a heavy rain. The heavier current triggers their upstream movement.

There are many false runs through the fall and winter. Some fish go upstream and a few days later they may return to the lake. Some fish will stay in the river all winter, and this is one stage of the spring spawn.

In certain cases, some walleyes will stay in the lake all winter while others head upstream. Fall rain will draw trophy spawning age walleyes like iron filings to a magnet.

One thing I like about fall walleyes is they are susceptible to so

many different presentations. Chances are, almost any angling method will work.

Fall walleyes are catholic in their choice of habitat. It can be a river, natural lake, one of the Great Lakes bays or a reservoir.

Now is the time to work up some autumn walleye fever. When the first cold weather arrives, many anglers concentrate their time and energies on hunting or watching television. Hardcore fishermen know that a walleye's metabolism slows down in cold water, and that is a clue for anglers — to slow down their presentations.

Photo by Gary Roach

This walleye was caught while using the controlled drifting or slipping method.

As walleyes move up a river, try controlled drifting or slipping to locate fish. An important autumn technique is to fish with a jig and minnow combination, and vertically bounce it off bottom while controlling the downstream drift. Start the boat in a downstream slipping pattern, and lower a jig and minnow rig to bottom with a 45-degree to nearly vertical angle. While slipping, try to locate where walleyes concentrate using a fish locator. Once a good area is found,

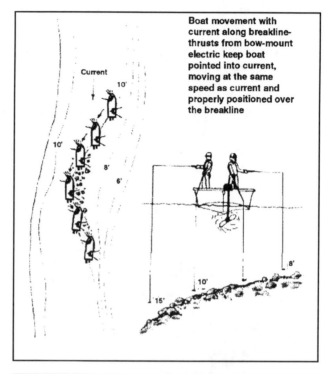

Boat movement with current along breakline-thrusts from bow-mount electric keep boat pointed into current, moving at the same speed as current and properly positioned over the breakline

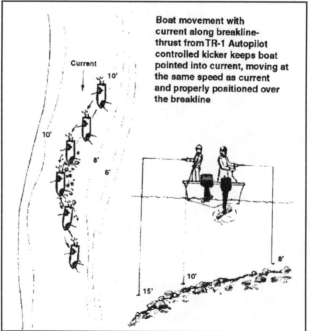

Boat movement with current along breakline-thrust from TR-1 Autopilot controlled kicker keeps boat pointed into current, moving at the same speed as current and properly positioned over the breakline

slip it a few times to catch the active fish.

Later, as things slow down, anchor off to the side of the area and fan-cast a jig and minnow, spinner blade or a countdown Rapala at a 45-degree angle upstream. Retrieve it very slowly along bottom, and use a slight rodtip twitch as the rig is reeled in.

In fast current, use a heavier jig or weight on the rig or crankbait to keep it near bottom. When using jigs start out using different fluorescent colors. Experiment with Berkley Power Baits or Northland's Screw Tail bodies on jigs. The soft body gives slightly more time to react and set the hook before a walleye spits it out. When using a jig, hook the minnow through the mouth and out through the top of the head so it will be harder to steal.

A plain, round, leadhead jig is fine, although a bullet-head Foxee Jig may go deeper a bit faster. It'll cut into the current with a lighter weight than when using a round-head design. Jig weight depends on the current — 1/4, 1/8 and 1/16 ounces — are my favorites. Heavier jigs are not inhaled by walleyes very well, and it's easy to miss fish. If the water is deep and the current is strong, it is important to use a heavier jig.

Photo by John Peterson

Slow trolling a rig or jig presentations are good ways to locate and catch fall walleyes in lakes, but an angler must be precise with his presentation. One way to troll with greater accuracy is to use an electric trolling motor and let the wind move the boat along the structure while pointing the bow into the wind with an occasional burst of power. This tactic will slow the boat so it is possible to work the edges of the structure or

 **169**

weeds carefully. Look for rock piles, weed lines, reefs or other structure that hold fish, and wherever possible, to work a jig or rig vertically..

Crawler harnesses like Northland's Float 'n' Spin are deadly. Build up a selection that offers Colorado and/or Indiana blades in different colors and sizes. A good place to start is with a No. 3 blade. Crawler harnesses can be used effectively in a lake or river.

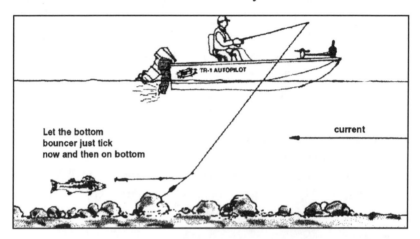

Let the bottom bouncer just tick now and then on bottom

current

When river fishing, use a Northland Rock Runner Bottom Bouncer because it will ride up and over logs or other bottom obstructions. Troll slowly upstream, and slightly faster when fishing downstream through holes. A faster speed than the current is needed to keep the spinner blade turning over.

A bottom bouncer weight must be changed as current speed and depths change in hopes of keeping the bait near bottom at a 45 degree angle. This is my search and destroy technique; it allows me to cover more water and find active fish faster than with a jig or live bait rig.

Remember that when fishing river currents, keep the snell to the crawler harness short. A length of 18-24 inches is best. A shorter leader length will causes these rigs to be pushed down to bottom where getting snagged can be a continual problem.

Fishing crawler harnesses around lake weeds may also create problems, but there are ways to get around it. Try trolling or control drifting with a bullet-type sinker or very small bottom bouncer ahead of the harness.

This rig will push the weeds aside rather than collect them on the hooks or line. When controlled drifting or trolling, let out just enough line so the rodtip can be dropped a bit from the striking position and still be able to feel the weight hit bottom. This will keep the bait about 1 1/2 to 2 feet off bottom. Continue to drop the rod tip frequently to maintain contact with bottom. The action of an arm lowering and raising the spinner up and down will often trigger a strike.

In deep water or near rocks and snags, a Bottom Bouncer will work best. It's possible to feel bottom without getting hung up.

Try to keep the offering just off bottom, but occasionally drop the rodtip to check where bottom is but don't drag the presentation along bottom.

Walleyes are light hitters. They tap a bait or lure, and if it drags along bottom, it is difficult to tell when a fish strikes. A fish will feel the baited lure jerking as it drags along bottom, and an angler is less likely to hook fish.

Randy Bandstra's walleye was caught using a bottom bouncer and spinner.

It's possible to pick up some fish while controlled drifting or trolling a crawler harness. But if they turn off from a crawler harness, don't give up. Switch to a jig and crawler or minnow, or try a jigging spoon. It is sometimes possible to start walleyes feeding all over again.

Leadcore line has played an important role in angling for many years. This specialty line is made of braided Dacron with a lead

core, and is most often used to take lures deep without having to use a lead weight. This technique works equally well during spring, summer or fall whenever open water is available.

This specialty line can be an asset to walleye fishermen, especially those who want to dredge the depths for larger fish. Leadcore line is usually marked in various colors, and colors changes every 10 yards to allow fishermen to know how many yards of line are needed to reach various depths.

Some walleye fishermen use segments of only three or four colors of leadcore line, and it is attached to monofilament line. That works fine for those who like that system, but my leadcore method is a bit different.

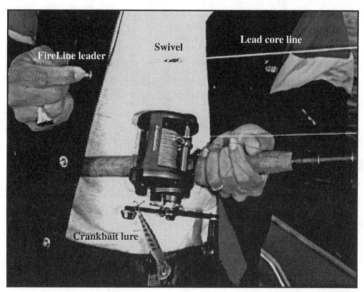

Photo by Jeff Wood

I fill a big Abu Garcia saltwater reel with leadcore line. It will hold 100-150 yards of leadcore, and line diameter is important to me. I prefer 18-pound Mason leadcore because it has the smallest diameter but the greatest amount of lead. This combination decreases line resistance to water, and increases the rate of sink. It sinks faster than any other leadcore line I've used, and it is strong enough to handle any deep-water walleye fishing situation.

Tie a high quality ball bearing swivel to the leadcore. This serves three purposes: it helps prevent line twist, makes it easier to join leadcore with another line, and it enables anglers to add a cross-lock snap so additional weight like a bell sinker can be easily attached.

My leadcore rigs have five to seven feet of mono or FireLine as a leader. The way to use it is to slowly let out leadcore line until the line and bait or lure is bumping bottom.

Reel up just a bit so the bait or lure skims along just off bottom. FireLine is my preference as a leader material when fishing areas with zebra mussels or snags.

If a No. 9 Shad Rap hits bottom in 24 feet of water with four colors (40 yards) of leadcore line, and the boat travels at 1.4 to 1.8 S.O.G. (speed over ground) on G.P.S., and the boat swings out over 30 feet of water to where numerous fish show on the graph, it's easy to slow down to 1.1 to 1.4 which causes the line to drop the lure into their face.

Another example will show how to raise the line and lure in the water without having to reel in. If you are fishing in 24 feet, and spot a big snag or big fish at 18 feet, speed up to 2.4 to 3.0, and water pressure on the line will force it up and over the snag. If the snag holds a big walleye, the change in lure depth may trigger a strike.

I can run bottom bouncers and spinners on one rod with FireLine, and the other rod with leadcore line and a crankbait, and it works well. I also can get a wide, slow wobble from crankbaits and still fish them near bottom.

Once an angler determines how many colors are needed to take his lure to a certain depth, speed control becomes the key. Faster speeds lift leadcore line higher, and slower speeds allow it to go deeper.

Leadcore line is a little known secret for controlling line and lure depth. It works anytime during open water, and anglers should learn this technique. There are times when it will put extra fish in the boat

It's important to try trolling along dropoffs and underwater humps at different depths. Make one pass and hit the top of the structure first because that's where the more active fish will be. Then work

down along the edge by letting out a little more line or adding more weight and make another pass farther down the structure. Try hovering over any fish located on structure, and work a jig or jigging spoon directly down to them.

Deep-diving crankbaits are excellent for working drop-off areas and other structure. Vary the speed of your retrieve and depth until a workable combination is found. Try a Roach Rig with live bait, and fish it along structure. Drop the rodtip to touch bottom with the sinker occasionally, and don't drag it around on the bottom because that creates a lot of mud. Try to feel the sinker tap

Photo by Mark Romanack

This walleye was caught along a dropoff with a Shad Rap.

bottom once in a while.

My favorite bait for walleyes is the red-tailed chub or creek chub. These minnows are hard to find at times, but are hardy and walleyes love them.

Roach Rigs should be fished with spinning tackle. Leave the spinning reel bail open and hold the line with a finger tip because it allows an angler to give feeding fish line as soon as the bait is picked up. The basis of live bait rigging is to let fish take the bait with no resistance.

Bait size and the activity level of fish will dictate how long to allow a fish to run on a free line after it hits. If the fish are very aggressive and small minnows are being used, try counting to 10 before reeling down to the fish and setting the hook.

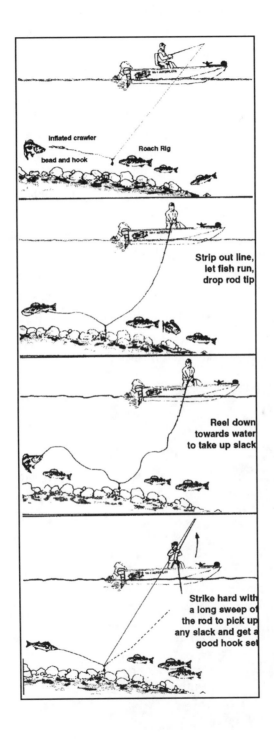

On the other hand, if walleyes are neutral and three- to five-inch minnows are being used, a wait of two minutes or more may be required before setting the hook. When rigging, walleyes will let you know how long to wait.

Once anglers find some fish, but they won't hit, try working a Roach Rig with a 5- or 6-inch chub very slowly along bottom on the dropoff or near structure. Allow a swimming minnow to provide the action. When a pickup is felt, immediately give the fish line. Give walleyes time to swallow the bait before reeling up any slack line and setting the hook.

I've learned over the years that certain places hold fish. Sharp breaklines out from weedbeds, the first major break off the mouth of a river, underwater humps or islands, and areas where the breakline comes near shore are all good bets when rigging for fall walleyes.

It doesn't make sense, but jigging spoons when fished aggressively, are killers for active and non-active fall walleyes. There is something in the way a spoon darts and flashes that will make walleyes strike, even when they've ignored all other offerings.

I rely on a few walleye jigging spoons — the Hopkins Spoon, Northland's Fire-Eye Minnow and Blue Fox Tingler spoon — for my action. The Hopkins Spoon works best on more aggressive fish while the slower fall of a Fire-Eye or Tingler can turn on the most tight-lipped walleye.

A school of freshly

(L) Mark Roach netting a walleye for Dan Roach caught on a jigging spoon.

Photo by Mark Romanack

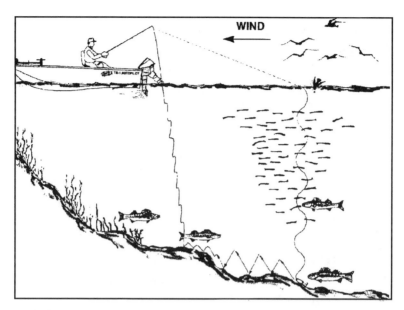

hatched shad are found all over lakes that hold these forage fish during the fall. Watch the birds or watch an Eagle graph for schools of these small fish, and then cast to the school and let the lure settle down through the baitfish. Walleyes often attack these schools from below.

Casting spoons into a school of baitfish is an excellent way to find active walleyes. When casting, allow the spoon to hit bottom (watch the line), and as soon as it does, snap the spoon off bottom and allow it to settle again.

It's important to learn to watch the line when using this method because the line will signal a strike and will alert an angler when the spoon hits bottom. This is why I use Trilene XT Solar line. It is incredibly tough, an important consideration when jigging spoons because it puts a lot of stress on the line. It also makes it easy to see the line, and the color doesn't seem to bother the fish.

Spoon fishing isn't a light-line sport. Heavier line allows a spoon to fall slower, and this results in more strikes. I use 12 to 17-pound test XT on my spoon rods.

My preference is a seven-foot medium to medium-heavy Berkley casting rod for jigging spoons. A stout rod helps me obtain the right

 **177**

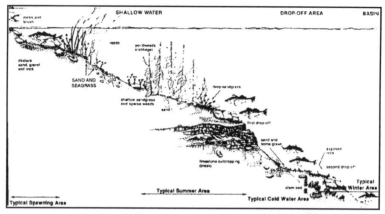

Courtesy of In-Fisherman

action from a spoon while it is an aid to burying the hook deep in big fish. Using heavier line means using a baitcasting reel like the Abu Garcia Tournament Series.

Rock ledges, dropoffs or other structure are ideal places to try vertically jigging a spoon. Flick the spoon up a foot or so at a time as the boat slowly moves along over good structure. Walleyes will usually hit as it falls; if the line remains slack or drifts off to one side, set the hook.

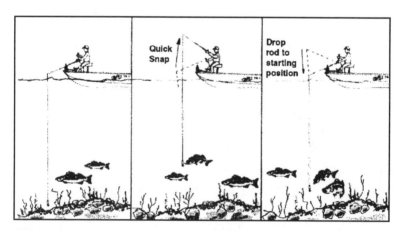

A 1 to 2-foot rodtip jerk every few seconds will work well at times. I twitch the rodtip just enough to lift the spoon off bottom.

It's important to let a spoon fall naturally. An angler doesn't want much slack in the line, following the lure to bottom with the rodtip will allow it to fall naturally.

There are times when the subtle "tick" of a walleye picking up the spoon can be felt. More often than not, fish will be there on the next rodtip snap.

In the fall, try a technique called "ripping" that can turn a normally passive walleye into an aggressive fish. Throw a Blue Fox Tingler spoon, Northland's Fire Eye or Hopkins spoon 10 to 15-feet into the weeds and let it settle. Then give it a good jerk toward the boat. Let it settle again and jerk again.

This method not only rips weed off the spoon but can drive a nearby walleye nuts, and they will hit it hard. The best spots are weedbeds near deep water. Once a single fish is found, stick around; because walleyes will usually be schooled up and it's possible to catch others nearby.

Photo by Gary Roach

Larry Allison netting a walleye caught while trolling along a weed bed edge.

A 1/4 to 3/4-oz. spoon is a productive size. It has the size and flash of a young-of-the-year fish.

Fall is a walleye feasting time, and the water is filled with small bluegills, perch, ciscoes, gizzard shad, alewives, bass, smelt and other forage fish. Silver or gold spoons are good at this time of year.

In early morning on stained lakes, a gold or brass spoon will work well. In the afternoon, shift to silver or chrome spoons. If that doesn't work, experiment with other colors or add prism tape or eyes to the spoon. Jigging a spoon through schools of baitfish can be a good way to catch nice fish.

It's possible to catch plenty of fall walleyes during the day by using crankbaits. Schools of young fish make walleyes very receptive to the swimming action of a crankbait.

These lures can trolled or cast along weedbed edges, dropoffs and structure in a lake. They also can be cast or trolled in a river in the head and tail of holes.

Try to keep lures 1 - 3 feet off bottom in a lake and just ticking bottom every few feet when fishing rivers. Set the hook hard on any little "tap" or hesitation. Troll upstream and down until you learn which particular direction works best that day, but remember that it can and probably will change the next day.

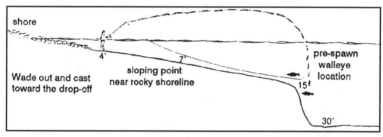

Courtesy of In-Fisherman

Natural colors are good when fishing in clear water on a calm day. Muddy water or rougher weather calls for fluorescent colors or a crankbait with rattles like the Rattl'N Rap or Rattl'N Fat Rap.

Anglers who are limited to bank fishing can obtain some great fall action. Locate an area with a steep drop-off to 15 feet or deeper within casting distance of shore. For daytime fishing, try a leech, minnow or crawler below a slip bobber. Throw it out into deep water and let it drift back in. Change the depth of the bait and/or bobber until you hit fish.

Try casting an unweighted, minnow-type crankbait or a big jig with a Twister tail at night in shallow-water flats near deep water. On a calm night, walleyes may be in shallow water.

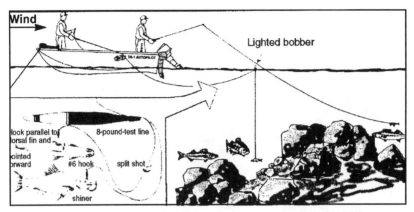

Courtesy of In-Fisherman

Rough weather will keep fish out along deep dropoffs if the lake bottom is silty or sandy. Walleyes won't enter real shallow water in rough conditions because sand can clog their gills. Remember to change colors occasionally until you find the magic combination.

A trick to try when casting jig is to cast it out and count how long it takes for the lure to reach bottom. Start counting along on each cast. If the bottom is a 10-count, and the jig stops at six, hit it. Walleyes most often pick up the bait as it falls.

If you live near a large lake with a breakwall or pier like those found along the Great Lakes, take two fishing rods along. Rig one with Blue Fox's Fire Fly lighted slip bobber, and bait up with a leech or minnow and fish around the edge of the rocks. Use a deep diving crankbait or shallow diver on the other rod, and use enough splitshot to work the tops of nearby rocks.

Remember those areas where fish are caught, and return to them later with a different lure. You will be surprised at the repeat business you can pick up.

Walleye fishing can be good until freeze-up. But that's another story, and it will be covered in the next chapter.

181

Photo by Larry Allison

Two walleyes that were caught four miles from shore on a rock hump by using a GPS unit.

Winter

Winter walleye fishing will separate the men from the boys. As a thick mantle of ice covers northern lakes, everything begins to change.

Cold water can make baitfish and walleyes lethargic. Food supplies dwindle, and finding fish can be far more difficult than during open-water periods. Anglers who catch fish consistently through the ice must brave bitter cold temperatures, wind chill factors cold enough to freeze the nose off a brass monkey, and slush or snow-covered lakes.

Once the ice and snow sets in, anglers no longer have the luxury of cruising a lake to locate structure with a sonar unit. But, with a little preplanning and preparation you can make winter days on the ice more productive.

Those hotspots that were found during spring, summer or fall may be just as productive during the winter. Or they may not.

Of the many spots that most anglers know about, only a few will produce for ice fishermen. And those will change as the winter season progresses. Anglers who can move from one spot to another will increase their chances of finding active fish.

Summer or fall months are the time to take the boat, graph and GPS unit out to record each spot in a log book. This will help them remember where each spot is located.

This kind of homework paid off in a big way for me several years ago. While fall fishing a nearby lake, I took time to mark a breakline for future reference. Once I got a look at the total picture, I noticed an area 30 feet long that jutted out from the main breakline.

This small "spot on the spot," was very subtle, but it rewarded

 **183**

me with two limits of chunky walleyes on first ice. The best part was that my GPS unit allowed me to go right to the spot and start fishing. If sonar had been used to find the area, it would have taken a long time.

Photo by Roger E. Peterson

This year, I can go right back to the productive area without having to guess or search for it. Think about all the other areas that produced walleyes during open water. A GPS unit can help anglers find that long rocky point, a sunken island, rock piles along the bottom or cabbage weeds near deep water. It hardly seems fair, right?

What to look for: There are many things to seek out when scoping out a lake as we prepare for winter walleye fishing. Look for quick tapering drop-offs, sunken islands rocky reefs, points, inside turns, humps, edges of weedbeds next to drop offs, etc.

Mark the best summer areas first, and then look for secondary locations with good looking structure. Indicate these areas with a way point and record them in a notebook. Like other technology, GPS was very expensive when it first came out and it was available only on top-of-the-line graphs. Today, Eagle offers small hand held units with full feature receiver/plotter at only a fraction of what they used to cost. They also are small enough to fit in your pocket and still do everything the big units can do.

Anglers who use an ATV or snowmobile for winter walleyes can kill two birds with one stone by mounting their boat unit on the dash and then use power from a cigarette lighter adapter.

GPS uses a network of satellites to pinpoint a location anywhere in the world, and usually to within a few feet. It is a great tool for finding a favorite summer fishing structure. Mine is used often to catch winter walleyes.

Bill Olar caught this walleye on Saginaw Bay in Michigan while fishing a narrow rock reef.

Walleyes love structure. This is as true when ice fishing as it is during spring, summer and fall. Any reef, submerged island, breakline or main lake point that produces during open-water months will probably continue to produce under a blanket of ice. Finding fish under the ice is a little more difficult though. Even if you use sonar when ice fishing, finding the hotspots is harder and it eats up more fishing time.

A GPS can be valuable, especially when fishing a large body of water. My Eagle GPS has been responsible for my success many times, especially under the time limits of a tournament. But, fishing trips only have so many hours and anglers need to make them as productive as possible. That's where pre-winter scouting can pay off.

While scouting, punch in GPS coordinates to save for ice fishing. Write permanent notes on a lake map or log book so you can match way points to the location, and don't forget to write down what type of structure lies below.

These stored locations should have their own number. I record each way point, along with its numerical longitude and latitude in a notebook (I guard mine with my life) so these numbers can be transferred to another unit if needed. This can happen when fishing in a different boat or when switching to a hand held unit for ice fishing.

If I plan to ice fish a lake or reservoir that I've fished before, I'll pack my gear, my hand held GPS and my notebook. The next step is to transfer way points for the lake into the unit.

Once on site, I load the sled, punch in the nearest way point and the GPS unit will literally provide a road map to follow. It tells me what direction to go and the distance to the spot. It even tells me how long it will take to get there.

If I walk at two miles per hour or if I travel on a snowmobile at 35 mph, it will automatically adjusts and provides an ETA (Estimated Time of Arrival). Amazing!

After I reach my spot, the GPS will give a Zero reading that tells me I'm on the spot. I'll drill several holes around the area, and examine it with a portable graph or a simple weight and line. Once the top and bottom of the dropoff (or other structure) is determined, I'll bait up and go to work. Even if the graph doesn't show fish, I'll give the spot 30 minutes before moving on to another way point. The reason I'll give a spot

(R) Linda Salem found good fishing on Saginaw Bay off shore from Au Gres, Michigan.

 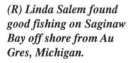

30 minutes is because activity on the ice (drilling holes, etc.) can put fish down for a while.

One nice thing about a portable GPS unit is that I can store any spot in it and make a notation in my book. This works well when an unknown location is revealed during ice-travel time. I can return to a hotspot after the crowds leave, and may find the fish still there.

The biggest advantage of this new technology is that it eliminates wasted time. I don't know anyone who likes to go through the motions of fishing without catching fish. Everyone is out there because they want to get in on the action. GPS can put you over the best locations without error in the shortest possible time, and it makes finding fish-holding structure much faster.

Never assume that winter walleyes always hold just off bottom in a lake or impoundment. The fish can be anywhere.

Photo by Bill Olar

A good auger enables me to drill enough holes in the ice to find fish along structure.

When ice fishing for walleyes, it helps to know the contour and structure under the ice before drilling holes. I like to start right up on the shallowest part of the structure, and then drill holes with my fast cutting Strike Master Lazer auger from the structure out into deep

 **187**

water.

My plan is to cut as many holes as possible because it increases flexibility. Winter fish can be anywhere, and this tactic enables anglers to check different depths. I usually start shallow in the morning, in 10-12 feet of water, and then move progressively deeper along structure as the day gets lighter. I reverse that direction in late afternoon and early evening. Don't be afraid to fish some deep (30-50 feet) areas off points or structure, especially during early ice but use extreme caution when doing so.

I once drilled a hole over a summer GPS location that indicated a group of humps, and when my Eagle Graph was turned on, it immediately showed some fish. Over the next three hours I caught five walleyes between three and six pounds.

Electronics also means using a graph for ice fishing. After a recent seminar on ice fishing, I was surprised at how many people have trouble using a graph. It's a little different using a locator through the ice than in a boat, but most fishermen pick up the subtle differences quickly.

If you don't use a sonar unit when ice fishing, you may be missing out on some great action. Just as sonar has brought major advances to open water fishing, so it has to ice fishermen. A quality sonar unit rigged for ice fishing can make hard-water angling more productive and more fun.

Choosing a sonar unit is as personal as picking a morning toothbrush. I cut my teeth on the ice with a flasher. Flashers work well for ice fishing, but over the past few years I've upgraded to a Eagle LCR. It took a short time to adjust to using this unit for ice fishing but now I'm convinced it can do more than a flasher.

Whether you use a flasher or an LCR, don't expect to just turn it on and have it perform to your expectations. Adjustment is critical to getting the most from an on-the-ice sonar unit. Anglers need to see fish, but you also should be able to see the bait or lure and its depth in relation to the fish.

The trick is in learning to adjust and read a graph. Graphs are not intelligent; They don't know the difference between a lure or a small fish. Learn to interpret what the graph shows, and the first thing to do is take the graph off automatic so adjustments can be fine tuned.

A graph on automatic may show a small fish symbol, making anglers believe they are over a small fish. In reality, it could be part of a big fish. Graphs operated on automatic will delete small details like a lure. If they show a lure, the machine will turn it into a small fish.

Contrary to popular belief, the fish ID options -- a setting that makes fish look like cartoon fish --, do not work as people think. Granted, fish may look like fish, but so do weeds, air bubbles, wood or anything in the water column.

Take control. Put the graph in the manual mode to obtain greater detail. A graph on manual also will respond and process the picture faster. Once the transducer is positioned in the ice hole, turn the sensitivity up until the screen begins to clutter and then back it off slightly. In the winter, turn it all the way up because there are less particles floating in the water. *(see picture #1 & #2 on following page)*

Another tip is to crank up the Gray Line to 30 to 33 percent. It allows an angler to better see the difference between bottom and fish near the bottom.

Last but not least, split the screen and hit the Zoom mode. One side of the graph will show everything from top to bottom, and if fish are just off bottom the zoom will pick them up. This allows anglers to look at only the bottom few feet of water or everything in-between on the other screen. With a regular picture on the screen, a walleye on bottom may be just a little hump of 3-4 pixels. But, when you zoom in, the fish suddenly shows up as a large image that is separated from bottom and in much better detail. It's like having binoculars under water.

If the unit is properly adjusted, and the bait or lure still can't be seen, a transducer adjustment is probably needed. The transducer should be perfectly level to obtain the best possible picture of what's directly below.

Setting the transducer level is a matter of trial and error. A tiny level like those sold in RV stores can be a great time saver. Glue the

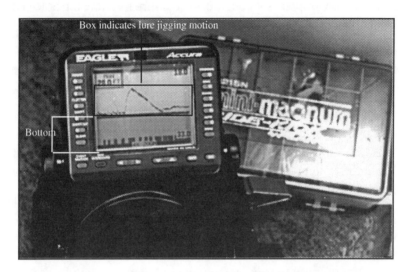

The graph setting is on full zoom. At this setting you are looking at the bottom 10 feet of water column and your lure presentation.

This graph is showing a split screen. The left side is set on zoom. The right side is a full screen showing from top to bottom of the water column.

level to the back, flat portion of the transducer. Another ingenuous device are those foam rings that float transducers in the ice hole. Use one of these rings, and you'll never have to worry about the transducer being level and you can easily pop it out of the hole to land fish.

Personally, I like a 20-degree transducer for ice fishing. It seems to work best under most winter ice fishing conditions.

It's important to remember that when ice fishing, anglers are stationary and the picture on the screen is different than the one displayed on a moving boat. Fish appear as long lines with some Gray Line under them. The bait, sinker and swivel appear the same but will be narrower with no Gray Line.

When a bait or lure is lifted, anglers will see the line rise. When the bait is lowered again, the line goes down on the screen. A jigging motion will make it look like a heart monitor machine.

When a flasher is used for ice fishing, adjustment of the unit is easier but no less important. Sensitivity should be adjusted as with a LCR. Note that little suppression button. Suppression isn't needed when ice fishing and should be set at zero.

Assume that all fish seen on a flasher or LCR are walleyes, and fish accordingly. I use my portable graph to show my jig, swivel ... it shows everything when my sensitivity, gray line and zoom are properly adjusted.

I can even watch a fish follow my lure up and down. They may be curious but inactive, and they can be seen looking at the lure before swimming away. Occasionally, there are times when anglers can actually watch a fish swim in and take the bait.

If active fish are seen on the graph, raise or lower the bait slightly to get it at the right depth. If the bait is at or just above the level where fish are seen, it's easy to be more effective than if the bait or lure is below them. If activity isn't seen within an hour, move to a new area. Sometimes a move of only a few feet will pay off.

Now, let's load up our equipment on a snowmobile, ATV, pull sled or vehicle (if the ice is thick enough), and hit the ice. Two other pieces of equipment — a GPS unit and a topo map — can lead anglers directly to the best lake structures without wasting time.

If I had to rate my most important piece of equipment, it would be a tough decision. I think I'd choose my GPS and a graph or flasher.

Fishing success increases as technology advances. As we near

A northern Minnesota lake produced good ice fishing for Gary Roach and his son Dan .

the 21st century, don't be left behind. A properly adjusted, quality sonar unit is a must where productive ice fishing is concerned.

When winter arrives, and water turns to ice, walleyes are usually on a feeding binge as they build up body fat before a long winter. Females need energy reserves for egg production before spawning can take place.

First ice is one of the best times for winter fishing. Walleyes are roaming the entire lake with a ravenous appetite, and anglers should be ready for them. Baitfish are plentiful, and most weedbeds are still green and healthy.

As winter progresses, ice thickens and snow cuts down light penetration into the water. Weeds begin to die and produce carbon dioxide instead of oxygen, and baitfish leave the area.

A fisherman must be willing to move from spot to spot to find fish. One quick check, especially late in the season, is to drop a weighted treble hook and pull up a weed sample. If it's healthy you may have a good spot; if it's dead or dying, move on.

Around first ice, walleyes are fairly easy to catch. They're still in a feeding mood, especially during the first few inches of ice. Be careful as ice can be thin in spots, and no fish is worth a 32-degree bath. Some rivers also freeze, but use extreme care to make certain the ice can support you, your equipment and other nearby anglers.

Walleyes can be very spooky, and ice noise can turn them off. When I fish near home, I like to get out the night before to cut my holes. I don't have to make a lot of noise the next morning drilling holes, and fishing can be much more effective. Avoid grouping tightly together with other fishermen, and try not to run around on the ice making unnecessary noise.

On the other hand, fishing on frozen rivers seems to improve if a little noise is made. That is doubly true if action has been slow. Noise moves fish around and hopefully places more active fish near fishing holes.

When fishing in a crowded area, try not to make a lot of noise because most fishermen do not appreciate it. If I'm fishing near a group, and the action slows, I will sometimes walk 100 yards or so away and start banging the ice with a spud. The action often improves and people start catching fish.

Several years ago a man with a gas ice auger walked into the middle of a group of fisherman and began cutting holes. The action had been dead for hours, and it suddenly picked up. After he stopped cutting holes, the action slowed down again.

I like to find the deepest river holes and concentrate my efforts there. The best times to fish are early morning and late afternoon, but if fish are active it's possible to do well all day. Usually, but not always, the absolute best time to fish rivers is that 30-minute period between sundown and dark.

River current usually dictates the fishing gear to use. I start out

Photo by Bob Bolger

Walleyes are found near the back of deep water pockets on the Saginaw River near Saginaw, Michigan.

with 8 to 10-pound XT line. If the current is strong and pushes the bait too far downstream from an ice hole, switch to a lighter line because the current will produce less drag on it. A switch to lighter line may cause anglers to lose a few fish but more fish will be hooked.

FireLine in six-pound-test is great for hooking walleyes. It gives lures more action, is less susceptible to current and few fish will break off.

Ever watched a dance floor full of people? It's a riot. Some folks just stand there and bump up and down. They do the same old thing, over and over again. Other dancers have been around the block before; they have a zillion dance steps to match their mood and the music. They move fast, slow and all speeds in-between.

Jigging through the ice is a bit like dancing except there is no music. There's an art to jigging winter walleyes, and it has everything to do with movement, rhythm and a swimming lure action.

It's fun to watch fishermen huddled together over a good walleye spot. One guy catches a nice fish and without anyone realizing it, the others are frantically jigging up and down. The excitement gets to them and they start jigging too fast and too much.

Stay cool and think about what the fish sees. Lures that are jigged

194

too fast seldom produce strikes because a walleye never has time to grab it. The water is very cold, and fish are lethargic.

Even on a good day when the bite is on, walleyes won't attack a fast-moving presentation as quickly as they will one that teases them slowly. Entice them, softly and slowly, and give them time to react.

Rhythm is important. Most people use a "lift-drop-lift-drop" method,

and it produces some fish. I prefer a "lift-drop-pause" technique with the pause lasting twice as long as the "lift-drop. Give fish time to see the bait or lure, to zero in and grab it. The key word for this presentation is pause.

This lift-drop-pause presentation should apply when using jigs, spoons, swimming lures,

Photo by Jeff Wood

etc. The "lift" part should be no more than six inches to a foot. Never use big, radical movements that move the lure one to three feet. After the "drop," hold the "pause" for two or three seconds to give walleyes a chance to home in on it. The lure, in most cases, should never be over six to eight inches off bottom.

It's a common thought among ice fishermen that lures should only move up and down. That's the way people jig, all day long, up and down, up and down. No variation. The only thing that may vary is how far the lure travels up and down.

Think about this. A nice seven or eight-pound walleye idling below, watching the lure. She's big, fat and lazy, and lethargic in the cold winter water. Something must trip her switch so she will react to the lure.

Most anglers don't know what it is. What if the trigger is not up and down? What if it's no movement at all or perhaps some other motion?

If an angler wants to catch her, they must determine what she wants. That means anglers have to experiment and change their presentation, which is easier said than done.

There are many ways to entice that big 'eye to grab the lure. Here are a few different lures and tackle presentations to try. Hopefully, one will work.

Always carry a wide selection of jig sizes, styles and finishes. Color, size and action can be critical, and we never know exactly what fish want until they start hitting. A boat load of lures isn't necessary when ice fishing. Carry a few favorites in a small Plano Mini Magnum tackle box in a pocket.

My box contains my main terminal equipment. It will hold several Northland Fireball jigs with double-barbed stinger hook attachments, There will be some Blue Fox's Bullethead Foxee jigs with Lip 'Em & Clip 'Em stinger hooks. I carry a variety of jigs and spoon colors in weights from 1/16-oz. to 1 1/2-oz. for still waters or river currents.

Photo by Bill Olar
Walleye caught on glow in the dark spoon.

My pocket-size tackle box also holds some Blue Fox's Tingler and Northland's Fireeye Minnow or Fireeye Jigs in several colors and sizes. There will be a few swimming lures, Northland's Airplane jigs and Normark's Jigging Rapala.

These lures are tied on at a line tie in the middle of the back, and they hang horizontally in the water. A fin on the back and sides causes them to swim in enticing loops when jigged upward. Use a ball bearing swivel, a foot or two above the lure to prevent line twist, and I recommend this with all spoons or lures.

Anglers also should carry a supply of single or treble hooks, splitshot and bell sinkers, swivels and cross lock snaps, and extra line.

The best ice fishing lures are made better if some "meat" is attached to the hooks. One of my favorite rigs, in deep or shallow water, is a No. 5 or 7 jigging Rapala with three small minnows, one on each barb of the treble hook, so they hang from the center of the lure.

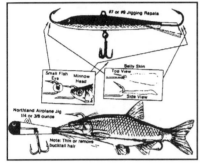

Courtesy of In-Fisherman

Northland's Fireeye Minnow also works well with a 1 1/2-inch minnow. Insert the hook through the mouth and out the back of the head so it will provide some tail movement as the lure is jigged. Removing the head from a minnow spreads more scent in the water, and loose particles of flesh will float around to attract walleyes.

It's impossible to know when the fish of a lifetime will be hooked. So, tackle should be strong enough and in good shape to handle anything that may come along. Use a rod stiff enough to set the hook in a hard mouth, and my choice is a Berkley Roughneck Medium Action ice fishing rod.

Quality line is important, and I like Berkley Trilene Cold Weather monofilament or FireLine in 6 or 10-pound test, depending on what lure action I desire Six-pound line is good for a natural fall; 10-pound is appropriate if I want a delayed, slower fall.

Ice fishing reels require a quality drag, and equally important is an easily accessible anti-reverse on-off switch. A drag may not perform as quickly as needed in cold weather so back reeling on a big fish may save the day on a big fish.

My Abu/Garcia Ultra Light has an anti-reverse lever on the back

where it is easily found while fighting a big fish. The reel also comes with a separate spool so line weight switches can be made quickly and easily for better lure presentations.

Rigging Tip-Ups

split shot

It's wise to fish with two rods or a rod and a tip-up if the law allows it in your state. It doubles the odds of hooking fish, and gives fishermen a better idea of what fish want on any given day. Once a pattern develops, it is easy to adjust.

For tip-up fishing, choose healthy, two- to three-inch chubs, shiners or suckers. Check tip-ups carefully to determine if the spool spins freely as a walleye runs off with a minnow.

A walleye will drop the bait if it feels any hesitation. Set the minnow 6 to 24 inches off bottom. I use one small splitshot six inches above the minnow and another about 12 inches above that so the minnow can move naturally but will stay where I want it.

When a tip-up flag goes up, walk quietly to the hole and give fish enough time to swallow the bait. Slowly take up line hand-over-hand until you feel the fish, and then quickly bring in the line and set the hooks in one smooth motion.

When using a tip-up, try to use the smallest possible bobber and attach it to the line. Once water depth has been determined, set the minnow depth so the bobber is just below the tip-up line spool. With a bobber, it's possible to tell if it was minnow, walleye or wind that triggered a release. Check the bobber location. A big fish will take line out, and the bobber will be out of sight under the ice. This simple test will eliminate having to reset or recheck the bait whenever a flag goes up.

Tip-up

Hand auger

Photo by Jeff Wood

It can get tiring to jig two rods at once. An alternative is to set one dead rod with a small Northland Fireeye Jig, and hook a minnow lightly through the back. Lower the line to a foot off bottom, and set it in a rodholder on the ice. Little vibrations of the rodtip are a sure sign that the minnow is alive, swimming and doing its job near bottom.

If the vibration stops, tap the rod with a hand or another rod to keep the minnow active. This method produces fish regularly, and especially during those slow midday hours. Always keep a dead rod nearby and within reach. Walleyes grab it hard, so be ready.

Here is a problem that often happens to novice anglers. A 10-pound walleye is hooked, and the angler is trying to fit it into an 8-inch hole through two feet of ice. The result is big trouble, and usually a lost trophy.

Anglers who are serious about catching big walleyes should use a large diameter auger blade. My solution is to drill two 10-1/4-inch holes that overlap each other. That eliminates jumbo walleyes from getting hung up on the bottom of the hole.

If I hook a big female that I want to release, it's easy to get her through the hole, released and back into the water with minimal stress or trauma. A gaff isn't required. There is only one way to cut this size of hole, and that is with a gas powered Strike Master auger. Other power augers tend to jump back into the first hole while the second hole is being cut.

One trick to getting a big, stubborn walleye up through two-foot-thick ice is to fight the fish near the bottom of the hole until it is visible. Time it carefully, and with a little extra pressure pull its head into the hole . Once in the hole, a fish can only swim up.

Be careful when handling big walleyes. Never use a gaff unless everything that is caught will be kept. Future fishing success depends on allowing big females to live long enough to reproduce; instead, keep a few eaters for the table and release as many spawners as possible.

Photo by Dan Roach

Gary Roach eases the fish up through the ice.

The first thing I do when setting up is to drill four or five holes for each person in the party. Spread the ice holes out throughout the area over good structure, and don't forget the edges and tops of dropoffs, reefs and weeds. Drill some holes over the bottom of the dropoff even if it is 30 to 50-feet deep. Do this and you'll be warm by the time you're done.

Once fish start hitting fish at a certain depth, stay at that depth for at least an hour unless a nearby angler starts catching fish in deeper or shallower water. If that happens, it's time to make a decision.

Show some courtesy while ice fishing; don't move in tight to another fisherman. Move shallower or deeper, but in the same line and depth as the person who is catching fish. And, above all, avoid making unnecessary noise.

If the action is slow during the day, fish right along the bottom at the dropoff's lowest area or where the lake bottom connects to the dropoff. This can be a hotspot.

Light causes movement. Early in the day, when the sun is still low, fish may be in shallow water. Walleyes are very skittish in shallow water under the ice, so as the sun comes up or cloud cover moves off, the fish will move to the edges, into the weeds or into deep water. That means anglers must move with them.

If holes have been drilled in advance, just walk to the new hole and start fishing without making a lot of extra drilling. When fishing with a friend or two, start out with each person trying a different lure and presentation. This can shorten the time needed to find out what the fish are looking for and can result in faster walleye catches.
Traditional jigging is the most common technique used to catch walleyes. A leadhead jig like Northlands two-tone jig, Fire-Ball or Foxes stand-up head, a flash lure like Northland's Fire Eye or Blue Fox Tingler spoon or swimming lure like the Northland's Airplane Jig or Jigging Rapala.

A little fresh meat will make a big difference when ice fishing. The taste and texture of fresh meat will produce more strikes and fish hold the lure longer which gives anglers more time to set the hook.

Laws vary from one state or Canadian province to another, but where it is legal anglers can use a whole minnow, a piece of cut up minnow or

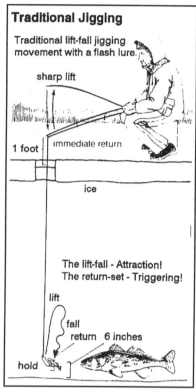

Traditional Jigging

Traditional lift-fall jigging movement with a flash lure.

sharp lift

1 foot   immediate return

ice

The lift-fall - Attraction!
The return-set - Triggering!

lift

fall
return   6 inches

hold

Courtesy of In-Fisherman

perch eye to add flavor and meat to an ice fishing presentation. Try adding a small minnow to each barb of the bottom treble hook of a Jigging Rapala. Lure size will dictate how big the live bait should be.

Drop the baited lure to bottom and lower the rodtip to the water level on a tight line. Raise the rodtip six inches and sharply lift it a foot before immediately dropping the tip. This causes the lure to flutter, fall or swim back down.

I jig once every two or three seconds, or five or six times in a row, and then stop to let things settle down for a few seconds. Then start jigging again. Strikes often come as the lure falls or just as upward jigging stroke starts again. Watch the line closely, and be ready for a hit.

Anglers will occasionally feel the lure being sucked in. Other times, the line will stop before it's supposed to and that is when a walleye has short-stopped it on the way down. Be ready to set the hook at all times.

Bottom skipping is much like traditional jigging except the jig or lure touches bottom each time The lure tapping bottom will stir up silt, sand or mud, and this creates the illusion of a feeding or injured baitfish. This technique works best in gravel or rocky areas.

Bottom-upping is similar to bottom-skipping. Place the lure at or near the bottom and twitch it up and down three inches at a time to

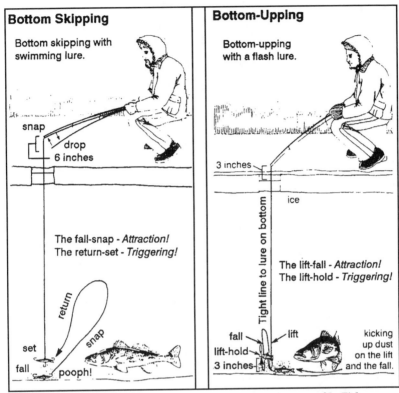

Bottom Skipping

Bottom skipping with swimming lure.

snap

drop
6 inches

The fall-snap - *Attraction!*
The return-set - *Triggering!*

return

snap

set

fall

pooph!

Bottom-Upping

Bottom-upping with a flash lure.

3 inches

ice

Tight line to lure on bottom

The lift-fall - *Attraction!*
The lift-hold - *Triggering!*

fall   lift

lift-hold

3 inches

kicking up dust on the lift and the fall.

Courtesy of In-Fisherman

stir up the bottom with a continuous motion. Keep the line tight and thump bottom. Pause occasionally, and allow the lure to lay on bottom or hold it just off bottom in a cloud of silt. This also works best in rocky areas.

Tight-line twitching is a more delicate method than any of the above. With tight-line twitching, lures don't lift and fall. Instead, keep a constantly tight line. Except for an occasional twitch, the lure just walks around in a circle over the bottom.

Swishing is similar to jigging but it has a side-to-side movement rather than up-and-down. Move the rodtip back and forth, from side to side, for three to six inches at a time. This causes a rocking or pendulum motion in the lure. It doesn't move up and down; instead, it just slides and twitches from side to side. Throw in an occasional vertical jig to add some variation. As in tight-line twitching, when a walleye hits the strike is easily felt because

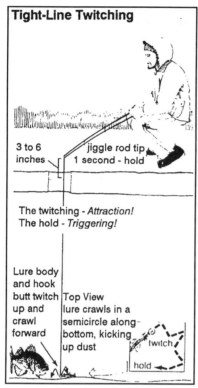

Tight-Line Twitching

3 to 6 inches

jiggle rod tip
1 second - hold

The twitching - *Attraction!*
The hold - *Triggering!*

Lure body and hook butt twitch up and crawl forward

Top View
lure crawls in a semicircle along bottom, kicking up dust

twitch

hold

Courtesy of In-Fisherman

the line is tight. This a great technique for beginners who have trouble feeling a strike with the more conventional jigging methods.

Jiggling will make a bait look like a nervous wreck. Move the wrist up and down rapidly one to two inches while slowly lifting and lowering your arm. Underwater walleyes will see a lure dancing wildly and swimming up and down, from deep to shallow depths, and back again. This is a good technique to find the depth of the fish but remember to pause occasionally at the bottom, middle and top of the stroke.

Mix these tactics up and have fun. An angler will be like a dancer who's been around and knows the steps. Mix and combine any of the techniques. Try jigging, skipping, bottom upping, twitching, swishing, and tight lining. Just remember what works and keep doing it. Who said ice fishing has to be boring!

With each of these techniques, just remember to pause and hold the lure in place. There will still be some movement, whether from the current, the line untwisting or just minor hand or minnow movement. Often, this subtle movement is the trigger that causes a strike.

Some of the buzzwords that anglers hear and read about can come into play during the late winter. Catch-phrases like "last ice" and "pre-spawn" affect fish activity at this time of year, and they can work to the benefit of fishermen.

Unfortunately, ice conditions begin to deteriorate because of increasing runoff and warmer temperatures. Be careful when venturing out onto the ice during warm spell, late in the winter when fishing near feeder creeks, streams or rivers.

Tributaries will draw fish in, and they can be a magnet in late winter. Try to put yourself in their migration path, and you'll find much more activity. One way to find these areas is to look at structure between the lake and the feeder creeks or moving water. Walleyes do not move "as the crow flies" from lake to tributary.

They still seek the security of structure like the edges of weedbeds, dropoffs, underwater humps and hard bottom areas with gravel or rock. This is especially true if there is a river or creek that flows out to or over the structure.

If the lake is well-known, or if an angler has a topo map, it's easy to plan a strategy and lay in wait for them in likely places. Once a general location has been chosen to fish, drill several widely scattered ice holes so everyone can move around until the fish are found. Spend 15 minutes in each hole, and move on to the next one until the action starts

Water depth doesn't play a major role in where to find fish. Walleyes are moving, looking for cover, and searching for protection and food as they move toward the tributaries. If ideal cover or structure is found at four feet or 15 feet, that's where anglers will find fish.

If anglers fish a bowl-shaped lake, more often than not the key areas will be weed edges, and over gravel or rocky bottomed areas. Lakes with structure like weeds, dropoffs, underwater humps and hard bottomed areas may mean covering a greater area and drilling more holes. My advice is to bring a friend or two and let them help locate migration routes that day.

Another hotspot, in more ways than one during late winter, are warm-water discharge sites near power plants. I like to fish such areas at night or during the day with a Count Down Rapala, Shad Rap crankbait or a Northland two-tone jig with a screw tail.

The best times to fish these areas are evening and early morning. There are times when walleyes will hit all day or night.

Many areas within two or three miles below a dam will be good

and the best places to try are in current breaks. Fish that migrate up the river tend to stack up below the dam since they can go no farther. Use a jig or crankbait near the walls and wing dams, and the base of the dam will also produce some beautiful catches.

Work these areas from shore or a boat. Try casting jigs or crankbaits at a 45-degree angle into the current and work them back with a twitching or pumping motion. Work deep, slow-moving runs and the tops of holes first, and then work the back sides of the holes near any bank with overhanging brush. Overhanging brush gives fish a sense of security and a lower light level.

Try the drop-back method with crankbaits to get in under brushy areas. Anchor above the area, and run a crankbait back into the area while working it back and forth and up and down. If that fails, try vertical fishing through the area with a jig and minnow.

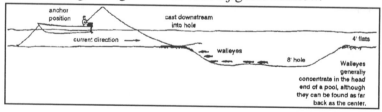

Courtesy of In-Fisherman

Always be careful of unsafe ice. Be aware of weather changes; a couple of days of warm weather can weaken ice. If there are doubts about the ice's safety, play it safe and fish an open-water areas from the bank or boat.

One more tip: always fish with a buddy. It's not only nice to know there's someone around to help if you fall through the ice, but it's fun to talk with someone while waiting for the next walleye to hit.

Photo by Kurt Beckstrom

Twilight can produce some fantastic fishing action.

It's also nice to have a witness nearby to verify your story when a big walleye makes her great escape right at the hole.

If warm weather arrives a little early, and the ice goes out, break out the boat and go after them. Use the same methods as when ice fishing but move out into a little deeper water. Without the protective ceiling of ice, walleyes seek the shelter of the depths as they travel toward spawning grounds during daylight hours.

Walleyes will still be found in shallow water during low-light periods of early morning, twilight and after dark. This is especially true when fishing gravel or rocky bottomed areas or riprap.

Try trolling with an electric motor and use a No. 13 floating Rapala with a splitshot two to three feet up the line. Work the riprap areas and dropoffs leading into the lakes and tributaries. Anglers also can try fan casting these areas with a Shad Rap.

Take advantage of the magic of the twilight periods. Walleyes, well known as light sensitive fish, will be much more active then.

One last thought for this pre-spawn period. Be selective about the walleyes that are caught and kept. Keep a few small ones for eating, and release the big female spawners so they can do their job to ensure the future of walleye fishing.

Tom Neustrom with and 11-1/2 pound late winter walleye released to fight another day.   **Photo by Gary Roach**

Photo by Tom Huggler, Outdoor Images

My wife Paula battling a night 'eye.

Night Fishing

Photo by Mike Avery

This Greers Ferry, Arkansas walleye weighed over 13 1/2 pounds.

My grandfather and father never used sonar equipment. Instead, they went out on Michigan's Muskegon Lake with 20 or 30 white Clorex bleach bottles, each one tied to 15 feet of rope with a small brick for weight.

They would drop a bottle into the water every 10, 20 and 30 yards in the area to be fished. The bottles would drift into the structure, and stop at 15 feet. The white bottles would show up fairly well, and if they weren't visible on a dark night, we used a flashlight to spot them from the bow of our boat We then knew everything outside of the bottles was 15 feet or deeper, and everything inside of the bottles was 15 feet or shallower.

That told us how many passes to let out on our level-wind reels so our lures would work just off bottom.

We took turns rowing with the wind to the end of the bottle line. We rowed out past the bottles, reeled in and then started the outboard. We would swing way out, come in and line up on our marker buoys, and start trolling again.

If we heard walleyes feeding with a sucking, swirling sound on the surface, we would stop and cast. However, if we heard jumping and splashing, we ignored it and kept trolling.

I'll never forget the night I caught my largest walleye. It was in November, just a week or so before Thanksgiving. It was cold, and a light snow was falling on a northwest wind. We caught several walleyes from five to 10 pounds, and Granddad decided to try a spot he knew intimately and where we didn't need markers. It was near a weedbed over a slab pile that was adjacent to a sharp dropoff.

It was late and we were ready to head in because I had to go to

Photo by Tom Huggler, Outdoor Images

school the next day. My Grandpa was on the oars, and we headed along the edge while slowly letting out 12 passes on the reel. All I could hear was the wind and the rhythmic whisper of the oars.

I suddenly felt a tap like a bluegill or perch hitting my lure, and I reared back to set the hook. It felt as if the lure had hooked bottom, and then the fish surged for deep water as I clung to the rod

(L) My daughter Rachael lost a little sleep to catch this walleye on Muskegon Lake in Michigan.

 **211**

and reel.

"Maybe it's a big flathead catfish," my father said. It wasn't.

The other lines were reeled in so I could land the fish. Five minutes passed, but it seemed to take forever. I wanted to see that fish ... bad.

"Be careful, don't horse it," Grandpa said. "It's a big walleye."

Suddenly the walleye appeared on the surface and rolled, lathering the surface to foam. It was one of those big walleyes that I had seen Grandpa and Dad catch many times, but things were different now. It was my turn! Dad slid the net under it and lifted my lunker into the boat.

Grandpa and Dad patted me on the back and told me it was a trophy fish. For a few minutes I felt much bigger and much older than my 12 years.

On our way home we stopped at a Muskegon Heights market to have my fish weighed. The scale finally settled on a whopping 14 lbs., 1 oz.

"Dad, can I have it mounted?"

"Oh, you'll get a bigger one than that," he said.

I'm still waiting to hang a "bigger walleye" on the wall. I'll just have to keep trying because they were always right when it came to fishing.

Night fishing for jumbo walleyes has been a big part of my family since 1929 when my grandfather, Smitty Martin of Muskegon, Michigan, began what has become a Martin tradition. He kept a daily log of his fishing activities for many years, and it served as the basis for much of what I know today about night fishing.

He carved and whittled homemade wooden lures that somewhat resembled today's Rapala, and he worked the lake from a rowboat. Some of these handmade wood lures were covered with aluminum foil from a cigarette package, and he glued the foil to the lure so it would produce a flash in the water as he trolled along dropoffs and points.

My father, Robert Martin, also of Muskegon, learned this night

212

fishing technique from his father. He and Granddad began teaching me their angling tricks sometime around 1964, and I've been refining those original tactics ever since.

I was the first in my family to use a graph and electric trolling motor to work various lake hotspots. Today's newer rods and reels, GPS units, sonar units and other equipment have simplified various aspects of fishing but an angler must still find fish.

There are many reasons to fish walleyes after dark. First of all, it's a hoot. Most strikes are fairly light, and every hooked fish feels like a monster when you can't see it.

One might ask this simple question: why fish after dark? The answers are easy yet sometimes difficult to tell readers, but part of it has to do with fishing when there is little angling traffic. Another is that fish are normally larger than those caught during daylight hours, and the third reason is because it's fun.

Make no mistake about it. Night fishing is different: the sights and sounds one hears or sees is unlike anything seen or heard during the day. An angler can find huge numbers of fish at times or much slower action with fewer but larger fish, and the fishing tactics outlined in this chapter have been used and refined by me over many years in many areas.

I'd first like to give some advice on how to choose and use the proper crankbaits for use under various conditions. Walleyes are versatile gamefish and anglers must learn to adapt to periodic changes as well.

A wide variety of lures will catch walleyes. My night trolling technique is built around using crankbaits. There are dozens of cranks available, and each one has its own time and place to be used.

CHOOSING & USING CRANKBAIT

Lure size: The larger the lure used, the larger the walleye you may catch. I once caught a 10-pounder with a 12-inch sucker and several small shad in its belly. That fish still came after my lure and hit like it hadn't fed for a week.

Crankbait lure sizes depend on what the fish are eating, but the

 **213**

question is, how do you know which lure size to use? The season may be a clue. For example, in the midwest where I live, crayfish molt in late June or early July, and are appetizing walleye tidbits because of their soft shells. At this time, use a small 2 1/2- to four-inch crankbait that is fat and round like a crayfish.

If gulls are feeding on concentrated minnows during the day, it is certain that a healthy baitfish population is nearby. At night, these same minnow schools will move toward shallow water, and trolling anglers often hear baitfish breaking the surface.

Move into the area with a flashlight and determine the type and size of minnow. Remember this cautionary rule: if you shine a light on the water, walleyes may spook from the area. Keep flashlight use to a minimum.

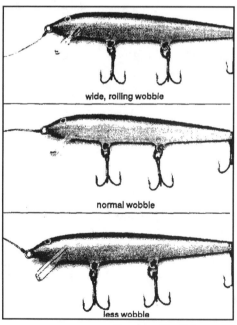
wide, rolling wobble

normal wobble

less wobble

Courtesy of In-Fisherman

When fishing a minnow type crankbait like the floating Rapala I do not like to use a loop knot which let's the vibrating eye of the lure rubs back and forth on the line and causes it to become brittle and weak. I use an improved clinch knot because it can be adjusted on the eye of the lure to change its action.

If the knot is down tight on the top of the eye, I'll get a very slight wobble from the lure. If the knot is at the bottom, I'll get the most erratic wobble action from the lure. I run them this way because of the greater flash and water displacement. The knot must be in a straight line with the middle of the body or it will throw the lure off balance.

To compensate for a accidental poor knot placement and your

line getting twisted up from the lure spinning, use a Berkley Ball Berring swivel about two to three feet up the line and put split shot above the swivel.

If the lake, river or reservoir holds mostly baitfish and minnows as its primary forage base, use a minnow-type lure. My choice is a No. 11, 13 or 18 floating Rapala with three No. 7 splitshot pinched on the line two to three feet ahead of the No. 11 or 13 lure. Use lures larger than the baitfish in that body of water so the lure draws more attention than the forage fish.

Lure action: A slow wobbling action will usually catch more fish than a rapid wobble. The way I work my trolling rod means I can get all three actions from one lure providing the boat is moving slowly.

Walleyes, like some humans, are lazy. They wait for any opportunity to prey on minnows, and they often hold motionless in ambush or swim slowly about and feed on unsuspecting baitfish.

It's important to keep boat speed down to one or two miles-per-hour. I use an Eagle GPS unit with a speed indicator to calculate over-the-water speed from satellite signals. These units can be an excellent investment if you don't have some other type of speed indicator. Another method is to watch floating debris as it drifts by. One or two miles-per-hour is the average speed of a man walking at a slow pace.

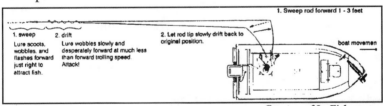

Courtesy of In-Fisherman

A night troller doesn't need a steady trolling speed. With crankbaits, move the rod tip forward to speed up the lure, and then let the lure's weight and water resistance pull the rod tip back toward the stern. The result is a lure that rushes along for a few feet, pauses, and then speeds forward again like a minnow trying to escape. This is called a dying minnow flutter or horizontal jigging. Fish hit when the lure pauses or settles back but they sometimes hit just as you pull the rod tip forward to impart lure action.

When using deep diving crankbaits for maximum results troll them very slow along structure holding your rod still. If you can feel vibration from the lure *you are going to fast.*

Slow down until you can't feel the action of the lure, then you have the proper speed. This allows for maximum wobble that can give you three different actions out of the lure in a very short distance. First a wide wobble, then as you pull your rod forward you get a short burst of a tighter wobble, and then drop your rod back to the original position causing the crankbait to stop wobbling for a second. Let your rod pause and your line become taut before pulling it forward again. This action can drive the walleyes crazy.

Lure color: In clear water, under normal weather conditions, a natural finish that resembles forage fish like alewives, gizzard shad, perch or smelt will produce best. To me, normal conditions mean clear skies, soft breezes and waves of under a foot in height.

My color choices under these conditions would be blue/silver, black/silver, gold/silver, perch (with a bar pattern), crayfish or rainbow.

Photo by Randy Bandstra

The splitshot rig strikes again.

In rough conditions featuring rain, thunderstorms, cloud cover, high winds and waves of one to two feet, water coloration and whatever light penetration there is in a clear lake will start to change. When this happens, use lures with some fluorescent color trim like chartreuse, orange or Fire Tiger. If this doesn't produce, try a lure like a Rattlin' Rapala or a Rattlin' Fat Rap.

In a stained-water lake, where it's possible to see two to four feet down in the water, use the same lure choices as in clear water. However, when a stained lake begins to turn rough or the sky is cloudy, use lures with fluorescent colors.

As waves build or the weather changes to rain or storms, try fluorescent lures with rattles to get the fish's attention. At times like these, anglers must compete against other natural noise so the rattles and high visibility colors are needed to get walleyes to see and react to the lure.

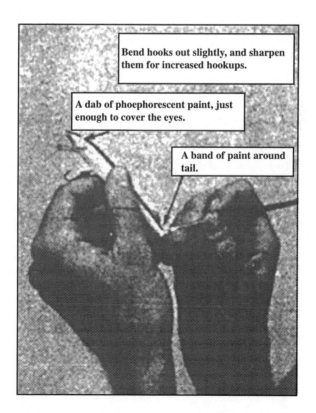

Bend hooks out slightly, and sharpen them for increased hookups.

A dab of phoephorescent paint, just enough to cover the eyes.

A band of paint around tail.

In muddy, turbid water under normal conditions, the best place to fish at night will be near bridges, docks and roadways where there are permanent street lights or dock lights that shine on the water. Rattles and fluorescent colors are good bets under these conditions. When visibility goes down, walleyes need something to zero in on and some noise can do the trick.

In rough conditions and muddy water, choose a larger lure. This will offer anglers increased action and more vibration which will attract fish.

Changing or doctoring lure colors is one of my favorite tricks. Some tackle stores sell tape in various colors for lure doctoring. In muddy water, use fluorescent tape to spice up your crankbaits by adding chartreuse or prism tape to both sides. To take this one step further, it seldom hurts to put some glow in the dark (luminous) paint on the eyes and around the tail.

Experiment until walleyes tell you which color or pattern combination is preferred. Color effectiveness can change from day to day, and what worked last night may not work tonight.

One reason why I started using prism tape and glow paint is because of my aquarium at home. It contains some walleyes, and I pay close attention to their daily activities.

They occasionally feed during the day or when the tank is lit, but when the lights go off and the house is dark, the aquarium starts sounding like a washing machine as the walleyes begin to feed.

I place shiner minnows in the aquarium, and once the light level goes down, the walleyes chase and feed on the minnows.

My eyes adjust to the darkness, and I can see the occasional flash of a minnow next to the glass. This walleye-prey relationship in my home aquarium gave me the idea to use prism tape and glow paint. It has made a big difference in the number of fish I catch under various circumstances.

Sound and vibration: As a lure passes through the water, it displaces water and creates vibrations that attract predatory walleyes. The larger the lure or the more violent the action, the more vibration it gives off. Vibration isn't the same as sound, but it works in much the same way.

In very muddy water with low visibility, use a lure with rattles to help walleyes find the lure. Until a fish makes visual contact and strikes, be careful because rattling lures can scare more walleyes than they attract.

There are no baitfish that I know of that sounds like a rattle lure. A crankbait that is too noisy may appear aggressive even to a big walleye. Work up to rattles only after trying other lures of various sizes and color combinations.

Lure speed: The best trolling speed is S-L-O-W. The most productive speed is as slow as you can troll and maintain some lure action. That usually means between one and two miles-per-hour. In windy weather with choppy waves, anglers can troll slightly faster. Walleyes are more active under such conditions and will move faster to a lure.

These guidelines may help but the only way to know is to wet a line and try them. Occasionally an angler will get lucky and hit the right place at the right time with the proper lure, but all too often, fishermen must work hard and experiment until we find a combination that works.

A Lake Erie walleye from Ohio waters.

Jimmy Lindner, In-Fisherman

 **219**

Several years ago I was on stage at the PWT Championship in Port Clinton, Ohio, and told the audience that a new state record walleye would be broken by a night troller. Sure enough, Angelo Zito did it three months later. When he caught a new state record weighing over 15 pounds.

Lake Erie charterboats are seeing clearer water and changing walleye patterns. Zebra mussels filter water at a rapid rate, and the result is those midday western basin walleyes often hit at night.

It can be spooky fishing once the sun goes down while trying to find your way on a dark lake. But, if you want big walleyes, the nighttime hours are the best time to fish. The trick is to allow your graph to be your eyes when precision trolling after dark.

Equipment needed must have several features. Between my Eagle GPS and a graph, I choose a lighted screen with a speed indicator and a temperature readout. They are critical to success, and are very useful for putting big fish in the boat.

One of the most important night fishing aspects to consider is knowledge of the water to be fished. Explore it during the day to find key structure to fish after dark.

In early summer, fish the edges and tops of newly emerging weedbeds. In big water like Lake Erie, look for structure attached to the shoreline. Examples include big islands like South Bass near

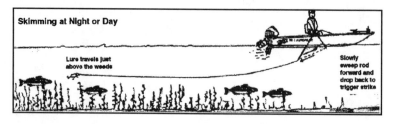

Put-in-Bay or a mainland point. Offshore reefs are not as productive as those near shore.

On smaller inland lakes, fish the inside and outside of weedbeds and shoreline points. These areas will usually be night walleye hangouts.

Once a good area is found, use a graph to locate any nearby

structure. And remember that night feeding activity normally occurs in water depths between three and 18 feet. Look for shoreline areas with a gravel or rock bottom. Dropoffs and ledges near gravel covered shallow areas hold fish.

Try to match lures to the conditions. My first choice is a floating Rapala four to seven inches long. Try trolling a No. 11 or 18 Rapala to determine which the fish prefer. I have over 100 cranks in a large Plano tacklebox, and will experiment until I learn which size or color works best.

Many people simply do not have as much time to fish as they would like. It's usually only two or three hours per week so they

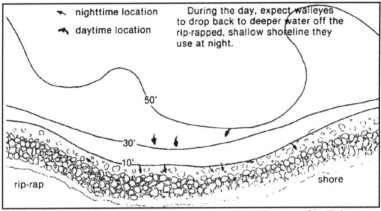

Courtesy of In-Fisherman

must make the most of it. The best way to waste that time is to troll unproductive water.

Learn your favorite lake and the various walleye moods, and you can zero in on the best locations and troll lures through key spots rather than fishing empty water.

Night trolling is like making a bombing run. Before you can hit the target, you must consider many things: water depth, structure, wind direction, lure speed and other factors.

Choose lures based on water clarity and the prevalent baitfish. Learn how deep each lure runs at the ideal trolling speed, and how much line to put out to attain that depth. Take time to test and experiment with lures before going fishing.

A formula I use tells me exactly where my lure is at all times. It's simple once you learn how to do it. Lure type plus line diameter plus lure speed plus length of line equals lure depth.

For example, through trial and error, I know that a No. 9 Shad Rap plus 10-pound-test Berkley XT or 20-pound Berkley FireLine plus one-and-one-half miles-per-hour plus 85 feet of line equals a 12-foot lure depth.

If I change lures, it will run shallow or deep depending on design. If I use lighter line with less diameter, the lure will go deeper. If I reduce speed, the lure will come up. Increase the speed and the lure dives (sometimes, with some lures, they just vibrate faster rather than diving). If I shorten the line length, the lure moves up in the water column.

Here is a hypothetical situation. On this night, walleyes are holding and feeding at 12 feet, two to three feet off bottom. That's where my lure must be.

It's important to run lures or bait past a trophy fish's nose if you want them to hit. Big walleyes are generally lazy, and will not go far from cover to chase anything. They conserve their energy and look

Photo by Roger E. Peterson

for feeding opportunities close to home.

So ... with that in mind, I'm ready to start my "bombing run," and my "target" is that small area called the strike zone. I know the fish are along the dropoff so I use only my big motor to get to and from a fishing spot.

However, when you troll at night, it's critical to be quiet and sneaky so I position the boat 100 yards upwind from the target.

I switch on the electric motor and let out the required amount of line, and watch my speed and graph while approaching the target.

By trolling with the wind it's possible to feel the slightest tap on the lure. The wind pushes the rod forward, and the lure pulls it back, so an angler always has constant tension on the line between rod and lure.

Since I'm trolling with the wind it is very quiet. I need little electric motor thrust to maintain speed and position. The boat responds well, and there are no waves beating against the hull.

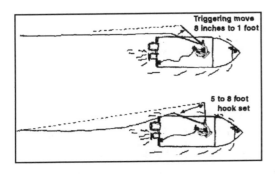

My arm and hand pulls the rod tip forward so the throb of my crankbait can be felt as it moves forward through the water. I then drop my hand back to make another forward stroke. This imitates a dying minnow flutter at a carefully controlled speed.

If there isn't a strike on the first pass, travel 100 yards past the target so the lure covers the structure's entire length. Troll a short distance off into deep water where walleyes occasional suspend as they wait for prey. Once you complete your pass, reel up and start the outboard to make a wide sweep around the area before beginning another pass. This helps to prevent disturbing any night-feeding walleyes that didn't strike.

Remember, the first pass is crucial so be right on structure with the proper speed. Wallhanger walleyes are spooky, and seldom give anglers a second chance.

This method works when an angler does everything right. A quiet, planned approach at the right speed, at the proper depth with the correct lure, means fishing on target. And that's the real key to catching big nighttime walleyes.

As long as a fisherman pays attention to details and can place lures accurately, it's easy to be within striking distance of the fish. This is far more productive than wasting time trolling through unproductive water.

A No. 9 Rapala Shad Rap, when trolled in this manner, is perfect when trolling in 15 feet of water. Watch the graph carefully, and stay away from water shallower than 13 feet to prevent hanging up on bottom.

The trick is to know how much line to let out. There is a simple method to determine line length with any reel. Here's how I do it.

Bait casting and trolling reels: I use Abu/Garcia baitcasting reels with this method, and they have a line keeper that moves back and forth across the reel spool so you can tell when you have made a full pass, and it may be three, four or five feet in length, depending on which reel model is used.

If, for instance, one pass equals five feet and you wish to fish with 60 feet of line out, it would require 12 passes to equal 60 feet. If, on the other hand, one pass equals only three feet and you wish to fish lures 60 feet back, it would require 20 passes.

Make a chart for each reel, and store it in your tacklebox or the pocket of a life jacket, and it will be available whenever needed.

Spinning reels: I use a similar method with my Abu/Garcia spinning reels. Tie the line to something firm, turn off the anti-reverse clicker, and backreel as you walk away. Count the reel handle turns, and measure the distance you walk.

My spinning reels lets out 22 inches of line with each reel handle revolution. That's all I need to make my own chart.

Never cast a lure out behind the boat and guess at the line length. It won't be accurate, and if a fish is caught, you won't be able to duplicate the same depth or catch more fish unless you are lucky. I prefer to make my own luck.

Anglers can increase the odds of catching fish by knowing exactly where the lure is when the first fish strikes. I often fish all night at only one depth, and a variation of just a foot can be the difference between catching 10 fish or being skunked.

Precision night trolling is a learned art. And right about now, some readers are wondering why such precision is needed. Here's the answer.

Ninety-five percent of the big walleyes caught just tick the lure lightly. The strike may feel like a weed hangup or a bluegill tapping the lure. Walleyes seldom strike hard.

A lack of precision with trolling depth means that anglers will forever be touching logs, rocks or weeds on bottom, or nicking the tops of a weedbed as they troll over it.

It becomes difficult to tell when you've had a strike. Or, you'll be so gun-shy from setting the hooks into logs, rocks or weeds, that a fish strike may be missed.

Precision counts for everything when night trolling for walleyes. If you have complete control over the lure and water depth, you'll know when a big walleye hits. You'll set the hook, and the rest will be history.

Good crankbaits are expensive, and cost $3-6 each. Some lure loss is inevitable, but anglers can control major losses by knowing how deep the lure runs at all times. Precision trolling can save $100 of lures each year, and that money can be funneled into other necessities.

Time is money to a walleye pro, and it's a good philosophy for pleasure fishermen. Precise trolling techniques mean more time hooking and landing fish, and less time spent trying to get snagged lures off rocks.

Trolling rigs require a medium-heavy to heavy rod because they

 **225**

telegraph strikes better and allow the angler to know when the lure is performing properly. A reel with a smooth drag is very important, and low-stretch line means firm hook sets.

My choice is Berkley's 20-pound FireLine on an Abu/Garcia level-wind reel, and a Berkley six- or seven-foot medium-heavy rod. For shore casting, I favor an Abu/Garcia open-face spinning reel on a six- to seven-foot medium-action Berkley rod, and my spinning reels are stocked with 10-pound FireLine. Anglers can get substantially more casting distance with FireLine than with monofilament.

Another advantage of FireLine is when fishing in zebra mussel-infested waters like the Great Lakes and tributaries. This line is tougher than mono and can withstand more abrasion.

Trolling crankbaits properly is an effective tool for extracting fish that hold on structure. It is a method dear to my heart, and over many years, I've learned to target structure with slow trolled lures. With minor modifications to meet existing conditions, I've used these methods wherever walleyes are found, and it works during all four seasons.

The two most important keys to crankin' structure are boat control and crankbait depth control. Of the two, boat control is what keeps anglers on fish.

If you troll a sharp breakline, and the fish are holding at 12 feet, you must keep the boat and lure in the proper area. It may not sound difficult until you consider that breaklines seldom run in a straight line, and wind and wave conditions mean boat control is much tougher.

I've learned some tricks to help with boat control. One is to use the wind to your advantage. I troll downwind whenever possible, and pulling rather than pushing the boat offers more control. When structure trolling, I use my Motor Guide foot-controlled, bow-mounted electric trolling motor to stay on structure.

My Eagle graph's transducer is mounted on the electric trolling motor, and I can see and respond quickly to any depth change. On the flip side, if I control (push) the boat from the stern with an electric motor and read the fish finder off my transom-mounted transducer, it's impossible to respond to structure changes fast enough. By the time the transom reaches the end of a point or sharp break to the right or left, the entire boat is so far past the structure that it's impossible to follow it.

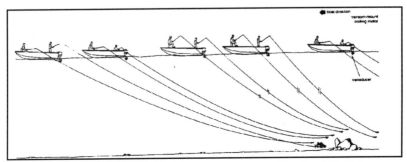

Courtesy of In-Fisherman

Stand and raise your rod if your graph shows abrupt shallow structures changes to avoid hanging up on bottom.

One little secret is to target structure walleyes with a No. 11 or 13 floating Rapala with three No. 7 splitshot placed two to three feet up the line from the lure. By slowing down, I can cause lures to sink deeper and by speeding up the lure will run shallower.

This works to my advantage when trolling the tip of a point. I speed up or hold my rod tip high when crossing a point, and then when I come down the other side, I slow down to allow the lure to follow the point's underwater contours.

Learn to let structure contours dictate which lures to use along a breakline. If the break is fairly straight, use the Rapala splitshot rig. If the contour is twisty-turny like so many are, use a deep diver like a No. 9 Shad Rap or a Rattlin' Fat Rap. These deep-diving cranks will reach depths of 10-15 feet on a fairly short line.

With less line out behind the boat, a lure will run straight behind and make it easier to follow sharp contours while keep the lure near fish.

It's important to know how deep a floating or diving crankbait runs, and it's never been easier. Dr. Steven Holt, Tom Irwin and Mark Romanack have written a book titled "Crankbaits In-Depth," and it tells anglers exactly how much 10-pound Trilene XT or 20-pound Berkley FireLine to release to attain any depth within that crankbait's capabilities.

I'd be remiss if I didn't cover one aspect of night trolling that is very important because it produces some huge fish. This method takes place late in the year before northern lakes freeze. Some hardy

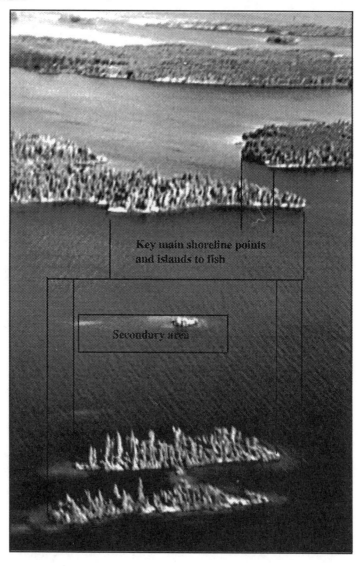

Key main shoreline points and islands to fish

Secondary area

folks will still have their boat on a trailer, and if you are adventurous, night fishing at this time of year can be very productive.

This is when walleyes bulk up for the coming winter, and they feed heavily. Big walleyes move into the shallows at night and are accessible.

Main shoreline points and dropoffs are key areas.

The sharper the break, the better the spot. Weedbeds can be great as long as they are still up and green. If the weeds are dying and sinking, the fish will be long gone. Scout such areas during the day, and then fish at night.

Big fall walleyes are opportunists. Because of their extraordinary eyes, they can see well enough to feed under starlight while prey fish cannot. This makes for easy pickings and fast fishing.

In most cases, night feeding walleyes will hold in shallower water than during the day. Walleyes that feed in shallow water won't tolerate an outboard thundering overhead. Instead, use a quiet electric trolling motor when stalking nighttime fish.

Many people, myself included, are in the habit of fishing a foot or two off bottom. At night, and late in the season, walleyes can be found three to four feet down over 15 feet of water. Or ... you can find them near shore in a foot or two of water.

In such cases, troll with an electric motor with a lure running just under the surface. Another savvy way to catch fall's nighttime walleyes is to throw crankbaits to the shallows from a controlled drifting boat.

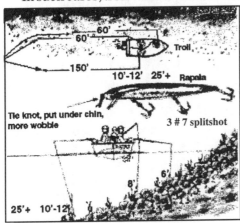

Running Riprap Rapalas

In any of the Great Lakes, inland lakes or reservoirs, channels, pier heads and tributaries that enter or exit a lake are good

spots to fish. They often have warmer water than does the main lake, and any current will attract a smorgasbord of small baitfish.

At night, walking and fishing the shoreline is a very productive technique. Use crankbaits with good vibration, and fish along shore or over the tops of submerged islands and reefs. This nighttime method is deadly on most walleye lakes, and shallow wading anglers usually get much better coverage than a shore-bound fisherman.

My method is to stay near the water edge while fishing, and enter the water only to net a fish. Full-time wading spooks fish near shore, but wading out to net a fish makes more sense than dragging it up on shore. The possibility of losing a beached fish is much greater.

The wader-clad angler must carry everything with him. This means a good crankbait selection stored in small plastic boxes, and the new and smaller Plano boxes are easy to use.

Wading anglers should carry a short-handled net, two pair of wool gloves, fingerless gloves, and a small flash light. I use a small model that can be placed in my mouth and held with my teeth, but a small light that attaches to a hat brim will do the job. Just don't indiscriminately shine the light across darkened water or walleyes will leave the shallows.

Hotspots for shore anglers are rocky or gravel-bottomed shallows near a dropoff. Walleyes seldom travel far from the relative safety of deep water, and often are within 50 yards of a dropoff or some structure.

Walleyes will stack up along a dropoff during daylight hours in seven to 10 feet of water, and then move in schools into shallow water as they look for forage fish after the sun goes down.

The best nights to fish shallow water in a sandy or silty lake is when the water is relatively calm. If the wind whips up lake silt, and sand is thick in shallow water, walleyes will not come in. Sand gets into their gills during rough water periods, so they stay out in deep water where wind and waves doesn't affect water clarity.

There are several ways to fish nighttime walleyes. The aggressive way is to tie on a crankbait and start casting. It's possible to cover a great deal of water with this method, and the crankbait's vibration will attract more fish than live bait, jigs or a crawler harness.

If you don't connect in shallow water, put on waders and wade slowly and silently close to deep water. Switch to a deep-running crankbait that dives to seven or eight feet, and keep casting. Good lure bets are a No. 7, 8 or 9 Shad Rap or any of the deep-diving, big-lipped Rapalas.

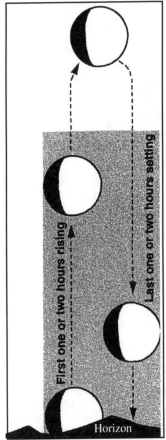

If there isn't much shoreline to cover, or you don't want to wade in the dark, try a lighted slip bobber like Blue Fox's Firefly Float. These little floats have a battery and light so they can be seen at night.

Use a four- to eight-inch minnow, set out two lines (if legal in your state), and relax while waiting for a walleye school to find the bait. If you catch a fish, keep fishing for another 15-20 minutes. Walleyes hunt together, and they may be others in the vicinity.

Another important detail of night fishing is the rising and setting times of the moon regardless of the phase as long as it corresponds with darkness. This is not an every night occurrence. Look for a moon chart that will help correspond with those nights you will be fishing. When this happens, if you are in an area where you are getting hits or catching fish, you are going to be real busy. If the area you are in is not producing, go back to where you had been catching fish or having hits. This is a short time frame that you have to work with.

Fooling big walleyes under the cover of darkness is a real thrill. And when trolling is properly done, setting the hooks in the jaw of a trophy fish is practically assured.

Once you've experienced the power and strength of a big walleye, and you've outsmarted him on his turf, you'll be as hooked on the sport as the fish on your line.

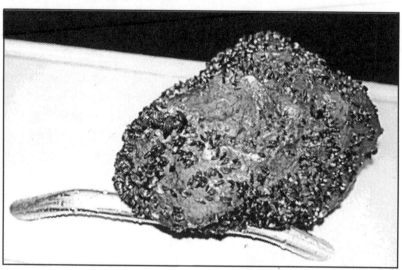

A light concentration of Zebra Mussels on a rock.

MARTINS QUICK
CHANGE NIGHT RIG

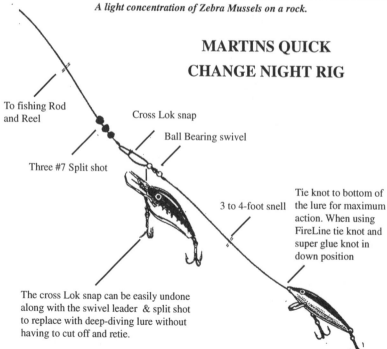

To fishing Rod and Reel

Cross Lok snap

Ball Bearing swivel

Three #7 Split shot

3 to 4-foot snell

Tie knot to bottom of the lure for maximum action. When using FireLine tie knot and super glue knot in down position

The cross Lok snap can be easily undone along with the swivel leader & split shot to replace with deep-diving lure without having to cut off and retie.

Sponsors

Sponsors are a necessary and vital part of a professional tournament fisherman's life. Without enough sponsors, a tournament pro must be independently wealthy to participate in a walleye tournament.

This relationship between angler and sponsor is one of mutual need. They need us and we need them. Sponsors never hand out money freely; the angler must earn his or her way in the business, and competition for quality sponsors is keen.

It goes without saying that manufacturers want to endorse a hot stick. The reverse is also true; anglers need the good will and generosity of each company. It's a two-way street that we walk, and the tournament angler pays his/her way in various ways.

Tournament fishermen are on the cutting edge of boat, electronics, motor, line, lure, reel and rod development. Manufacturers need people to help develop new and better angling equipment while we depend on them for endorsements that enable us to continue fishing. One hand washes the other, and that is as it should be because it's impossible to win enough fishing tournament money to make a decent living.

These companies enable me to pursue my dream of fishing in walleye tournaments, make a living and produce this book. In return, I help them develop new products or produce new and innovative tackle changes that help anglers enjoy fishing.

The following are my sponsors, and without them, this book and my way of life wouldn't be possible. To each and every one, a heartfelt Thank You!

Abu Garcia (fishing reels); Berkley (rods, line, PowerBaits); Blue Fox (jigs, spinners, spoons); Church Tackle (Mr. Walleye planer boards); Cobra Marine (cavitation plate); Costa Del Mar (sunglasses); Eagle Electronics (GPS & sonar units); Fishing Hotspots (lake & river maps); Gage Motor Mall (Suburban dealer); Gary Roach's Favorites (fish coating & batter mixes); Lund (boats); Mariner (outboard motors); Matteson Marine (boat dealer); MotorGuide (electric trolling motors); Muskegon Awning (boat covers & ice shanty); Normark (lures & fillet knives); Northland Fishing Tackle (jigs, rigs & terminal tackle); Ocean Systems Splash Cam (underwater camera); Plano (tackle boxes); Round-a-Mount (RAM mounts for antennas, electric motors, electronics & rods); Scent-Lok (odor-free hunting clothes); Simpson Lawrance Offshore Plastimo Compass; Strike Master (ice auger); TR-1 Nautamatic Marine (auto pilot); TrailMaster Trailers (boat trailer); Tru-Turn/Daiichi (hooks); UltraRide(adjustable boat seats); and Wave Wacker (water deflection devices).

For a Lifetime of Fishing
and The Fish of a Lifetime!

Ambassadeur
6500 C3

Cardinal

for life.

TRILENE IS STRONGER!

 We've proven it in the lab. You've proven it on the water. Trilene® is up to 30% stronger than Stren.® That's why Berkley® Trilene is America's #1 fishing line. *It's Super Strong!*™

Berkley®
©1996 Berkley, Inc.
Dedicated to the Future of Fishing℠

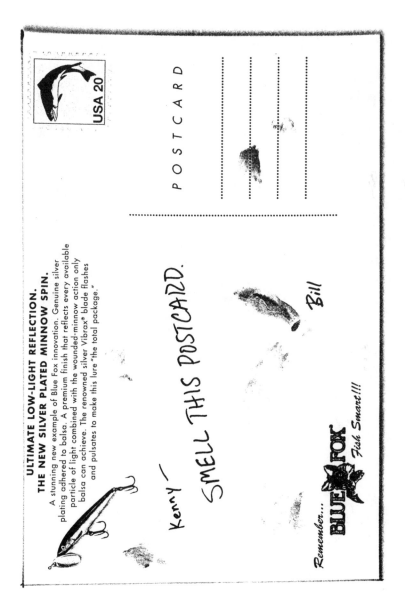

ULTIMATE LOW-LIGHT REFLECTION.
THE NEW SILVER PLATED MINNOW SPIN.

A stunning new example of Blue Fox innovation. Genuine silver plating adhered to balsa. A premium finish that reflects every available particle of light combined with the wounded-minnow action only balsa can achieve. The renowned silver Vibrax® blade flashes and pulsates to make this lure "the total package."

Kerry —

SMELL THIS POSTCARD.

Bill

Remember...

BLUE FOX
Fish Smart!!!

POSTCARD

USA 20

237

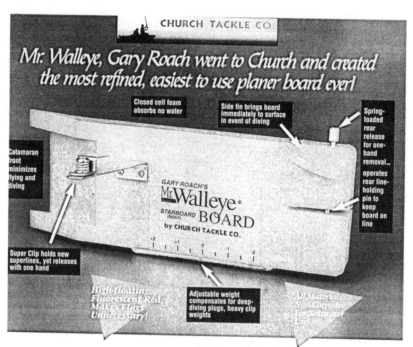

CHURCH TACKLE CO.

Mr. Walleye, Gary Roach went to Church and created the most refined, easiest to use planer board ever!

Closed cell foam absorbs no water

Side fin brings board immediately to surface in event of diving

Spring-loaded rear release for one-hand removal... operates rear line-holding pin to keep board on line

Catamaran front minimizes flying and diving

GARY ROACH'S
Mr. Walleye®
STARBOARD **BOARD**
(RIGHT)
by CHURCH TACKLE CO.

Super Clip holds new superlines, yet releases with one hand

High-floating Fluorescent Red Makes Flags Unnecessary!

Adjustable weight compensates for deep-diving plugs, heavy clip weights

All Materials Non-Corrosive For Saltwater Use!

hen one of the world's greatest fishing professionals Gary Roach came to us with an idea for an in-line planer board design, *we listened.* **Then we built the world's greatest planer board!**

"I wanted a board that was the best!"

Consider these features:

• A lightweight, metal clip that's coated with a material NASA uses in the space shuttle program. The clip holds the new, ultra thin, slippery braids and fused lines (like Berkley FireLine) that are popular for trolling. Set correctly, this clip won't damage even light monofilament. It's designed so the board can be removed with just one hand while fighting a fish.

• A spring-loaded retaining pin holds the line in a groove at the rear of the board. Just pull the pin with one hand when removing the board. Anglers after hard-charging fish like salmon, stripers and saltwater species may set the Super Clip light enough so that strikes pull the line free; the pin holds the board on the line as it slides back to a swivel tied a few feet in front of the lure.

• An adjustable keel weight keeps the nose of the board tracking in the water even when using deep-diving plugs or heavy weights.

• Closed-cell foam flotation absorbs no water.

• The board's catamaran shape minimizes diving and flying when trolling upwind or hitting a large wave at higher speeds. If the board does dive, a side fin on the rear of the board immediately planes the board back to the surface.

• Made in USA of non-corrosive materials suitable for saltwater use.

CHURCH TACKLE CO.
7075 Hillandale Rd.
Sodus, MI 49126
616-934-8528

Pro Series
Boat Planing Stabilizers

CoBra Marine Co.

1). Enhances The Performance Built Into Every Boat

•→ CoBra Stabilizers Are In Use On Boats Ranging From
- Professional Tunnel Hull Drags
- 16 to 34 foot Single & Twin I/O
- Walleye, Bass & Flats Boats
- State & Water Rescue
- Bay / Skiffs • Inflatables

2). How Do They Work? Hi-Performance Principles Of HydroDynamic Force Transfer •• No Aerodynamics ••

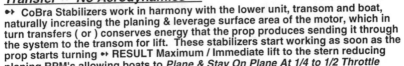

THE EDGE Pro Series

•→ CoBra Stabilizers work in harmony with the lower unit, transom and boat, naturally increasing the planing & leverage surface area of the motor, which in turn transfers (or) conserves energy that the prop produces sending it through the system to the transom for lift. These stabilizers start working as soon as the prop starts turning •• RESULT Maximum / Immediate lift to the stern reducing planing RPM's allowing boats to *Plane & Stay On Plane At 1/4 to 1/2 Throttle Essential for Tolling Or Back Trolling*, combined with *Whip Cracking Hole Shots and Super Low On Plane Speeds.*

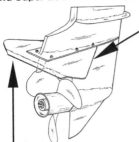

Professional Quality Marine Grade 304 Satin Stainless Steel Or Hi-Temp Powder Coated Alloy •→ CoBra Pro Series Planing Stabilizers Set The Industry Standard For Ultimate Quality, Durability and Factory Appearance.

Performance Technology That *EXCEEDS* The Adverse Tournament Conditions & Tough Standards Set By Top Professionals Like

Mounts *UNDER* The Cavitation Plate On Outboards & I/O's *Eliminating Stress & Breakage To The Lower Unit Casting*

MARK MARTIN

See Your Local Dealer
- Or Contact -
CoBra Marine Co. P. O. Box 483 Grover, MO 63040 • 314-458-2480

AMERICA'S NUMBER ONE
POLARIZED SUNGLASSES™!

Costa Del Mar is the name you have known and trusted for over 15 years to provide you the finest in Polarized sunglasses. Their optically correct lenses plus the exclusive Costa Del Mar Colorific Polarization System™ combine to give you 100% UV protection, 100% polarization*, and the greatest visual acuity available. Add to that the Costa Del Mar Lifetime Warranty and you have timeless beauty, function, and craftsmanship which is unequaled. What else would you expect from America's Number One Polarized Sunglasses™.

*Independent Laboratory Certified

PRESCRIPTION SERVICE AVAILABLE
123 N. Orchard • Ormond Beach, FL 32174
800-447-3700 • FAX 904-677-3737 • www.costadelmar.com

America's #1 Polarized Sunglasses™

THE REASONS TO OWN EAGLE SONAR ARE NOW EVEN CLEARER.

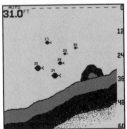

With a 160 x 160 pixel screen, Ultra Classic™ sports a higher display resolution and better graphics detail than most units costing twice as much.

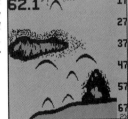

With an unbelievably detailed 240 x 240 pixel, Film SuperTwist display, Optima™ boasts the highest screen resolution in the history of Eagle sonar.

Successful Fishing Made Simple

http://www.eaglesonar.com

 **241**

Fishing Hot Spots.

FHS Maps™

America's Fishing Map

From Lake of the Woods, Ontario, to Lake Okeechobee, Florida, **Fishing Hot Spots**® offers the nation's largest selection of quality fishing maps.

FHS has over 500 maps, including the most popular walleye waters in the country....

Bay of Quinte, ONT	Little Bay de Noc, MI
Big Bay de Noc, MI	McConaughy, NE
Big Stone Lake, MN/SD	Mille Lacs, MN
Cass Lake/Pike Bay, MN	Mississippi River
Chautauqua, NY	Lake Oahe, SD
Chippewa Flowage, WI	Lake Okoboji, IA
Detroit River, MI	Oneida Lake, NY
Eagle Lake, ONT	Lake Ontario, NY
Lake Erie, OH/MI	Petenwell Flowage,WI
Gogebic, MI	Saginaw Bay, MI
Green Bay, WI	St.Clair, MI
Greers Ferry, AR	Vermilion Lake, MN
Kabetogama, MN	Winnebago, WI
Lake of the Woods, ONT	Winnibigoshish, MN
Leech Lake, MN	Wisconsin River, WI

Fishing Hot Spots Maps...
Maps so good you'll ask for them by name

Available at bait & tackle shops and sporting goods dealers or call: 1-800-ALL-MAPS.

Internet www.fishingmaps.com

GET HOOKED...
better reel into Gage!

Experience the
Gage advantage.

- Knowledgeable Service Representatives
- Factory Trained Mechanics
- Latest Automotive Service Technology
- Genuine Factory Parts

GAGE MOTOR MALL

Customer Support Program

842-2250 • (800) 886-7227
Beacon (US-31) • GRAND HAVEN • N. of Robbins
Open daily 9 - 6, Mon. & Thur. 'til 8, Sat. 9 - 1

243

Gary Roach's

𝔽𝕒𝕧𝕠𝕣𝕚𝕥𝕖™

Coating & Batter Mix!

FISHING EDUCATOR

* Fishing Hall of Famer

* "92 P.W.T. Angler of the Year!

* Gary Roach's
   Favorite Coating
   & Batter Mixes

* Seminars

* Books

* And More!

Distributed by:

Mr. Walleye™ Specialties, Inc.

Call or write:
Mark Martin
P.O.B. 103
Twin Lake, MI 49457
616-744-0330

Nothing Even Comes Close!

On the water, there is nothing that compares to a Lund. They've got smarter fishing features. The smoothest ride. The best engineered construction. Superior safety. Ultra comfort. And a legendary level of performance that's not only the best thing on water today, but also seems to improve with age. That's why Lunds hold their value better than any other boat. And that's why the average Lund owner has owned four and why nearly nine out of ten Lund owners will tell you they'd buy a Lund again.

Whether you're looking for your first Lund or thinking of trading up, you simply can't go wrong in one of these extraordinary fishing machines. Talk to any Lund owner you see and they'll tell you. Nothing comes close to a Lund.

Call 218-385-2235
for your nearest Lund dealer.

©1998 Lund Boats, A Genmar® Company, P.O. Box 248, New York Mills, MN 56567

Mariner 9.9 Four Stroke

☑ **Whisper Quiet**
without sacrificing
performance

☑ **Burns Less Fuel**
40% less fuel
consumption – giving
extraordinary value to
the user

☑ **Incredibly Clean**
with no smoke

☑ **No Mixing**
gas and oils

*Get your Hands
on a 4-Stroke!*

MARINER OUTBOARDS

Mariner Outboards are products of Mercury Marine.

246

Matteson Marine.

Your Complete Marine Headquarters
SALES & SERVICE

TRAILMASTER   *minn kota*

Johnson OUTBOARDS   **MERCURY OUTBOARDS**

•Hurricane •Sweetwater •Aqua Patio
•Sanpan •Shorelander •Shore Station
•Storage •Rental •Slip Rental •Lund
Located on Gun Lake

672-5292
12001 MARSH RD., GUN LAKE

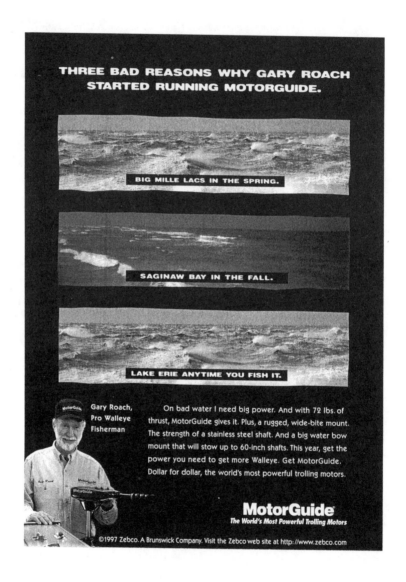

THREE BAD REASONS WHY GARY ROACH
STARTED RUNNING MOTORGUIDE.

BIG MILLE LACS IN THE SPRING.

SAGINAW BAY IN THE FALL.

LAKE ERIE ANYTIME YOU FISH IT.

Gary Roach,
Pro Walleye
Fisherman

On bad water I need big power. And with 72 lbs. of thrust, MotorGuide gives it. Plus, a rugged, wide-bite mount. The strength of a stainless steel shaft. And a big water bow mount that will stow up to 60-inch shafts. This year, get the power you need to get more Walleye. Get MotorGuide. Dollar for dollar, the world's most powerful trolling motors.

MotorGuide
The World's Most Powerful Trolling Motors

©1997 Zebco. A Brunswick Company. Visit the Zebco web site at http://www.zebco.com

Muskegon Awning

Where we make fishing and other outdoor sports a four-season possibility with: the Lodge ice fishing system, the Ultiblind four-season blind, and many other Multisport Products.

Best of luck with the new book, Mark.

1-800-968-3686

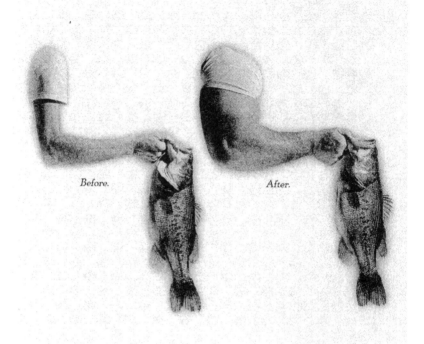

Before.   After.

Amazing results in just one summer.

The Legendary Finnish Minnow.

"Rattlin'"

BUCK-SHOT® RATTLE JIG

"The Racket Rattles 'Em Up!"

The BUCK-SHOT® RATTLE JIG thumps, ticks, clicks and clatters ... ringing the dinner bell to all game fish!

New

Eagle-Claw® "lazer-sharp" hook!

"Double-barb" bait-holding collar!

Buck-shot "rattle-shell" emits rattlin' sound vibrations!

Flexible silicone "rattle-band" ring!

"Wedge" head design!

Deadly on Perch, Crappie, Walleye & Bass!

SPECIAL OFFER: For more information, call or write for my NORTHLAND FISHERMAN ... catalog & fishing "secrets" booklet. IT'S FREE.

Northland FISHING TACKLE
3209 MILL STREET N.E. / BEMIDJI, MINNESOTA 56601

"Sonic"

WHISTLER® PROPELLER JIG

"The Jig ... Fish Can Hear!"

The WHISTLER® JIG adds flash and sonic vibration to attract fish and trigger strikes. Just rig it ... and jig it!

IT'S HOT!

Eagle-Claw® "lazer-sharp" fish hook!

Bait-collar holds live-bait & plastic trailers!

Hollow metallic bead transmits "whistling" sound to trigger strikes!

Propeller blade flashes & creates vibrations to attract fish!

Deadly on Perch, Crappie, Walleye & Bass!

SPECIAL OFFER: For more information, call or write for my NORTHLAND FISHERMAN ... catalog & fishing "secrets" booklet. IT'S FREE.

Northland FISHING TACKLE
3209 MILL STREET N.E. / BEMIDJI, MINNESOTA 56601

"Sonic"

RATTLIN' RAINBOW

"It Shakes, Rattles and Rolls!"

The RATTLIN' RAINBOW SPIN-NER attracts fish with thumping sound vibration! They are dynamite in stained, colored and muddy water!

New

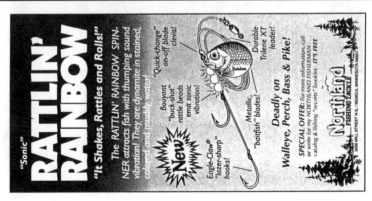

Bouyant "buck-shot" rattle beads emit sonic vibration!

"Quick-change" on-off blade clevis!

Durable Trilene XT leader!

Metallic, "baitfish" blades!

Eagle-Claw® "lazer-sharp" hooks!

Deadly on Walleye, Perch, Bass & Pike!

SPECIAL OFFER: For more information, call or write for my NORTHLAND FISHERMAN ... catalog & fishing "secrets" booklet. IT'S FREE.

Northland FISHING TACKLE
3209 MILL STREET N.E. / BEMIDJI, MINNESOTA 56601

"A place for everything, & everything in its place"
Mom

"Regardlesss of the technique I use to find and catch fish, I keep my tackle organized & carry it all in my *Plano Tackle System*™"

Mark Martin
Professional Walleye Angler

Looking for the perfect model of efficiency? Look no further than the Plano Tackle System Display at your favorite retailer. It's the ultimate way to organize, transport, and access all your valuable tackle.

No other system allows you to mix and match components as easily. So you can take with you exactly what you need, and no more. Plus, all Plano and Tackle Logic components are made to last with the highest quality materials. So your system will be working for you a long, long time.

THE SYSTEM WORKS

$3⁰⁰ REBATE

Purchase a Model #1234 Guide Series™ system and recieve $3.00 back from Plano Tackle Systems®

PLANO
TACKLE SYSTEMS

GUIDE series

Send Product Label and Reciept to:
Plano Rebate Offer • 217 S. West Street • Sandwich, IL • 60548

Offer ends December 31st, 1998

Rig Your Boat Like Top Walleye & BASS Pros Do!

Mark Martin

Gary Roach

R-A-M
Mounting Systems®
Patented & Pat. Pend.

Round-A-Mount is the new ball and socket mounting system that allows you to mount practically anything anywhere. Whether you need to mount a sonar, GPS, camera, light, computer, cell phone, mirror, antenna, or just about anything else in a boat, aircraft, vehicle, ATV, snowmobile or other situation R-A-M's family of over 130 interchangeable accessories offers solutions to your most challenging mounting problems. It's unique design provides easy installation, mobility, versatility, vibration protection and durability. For strength and corrosion resistance, R-A-M's made of marine grade aluminum with a powder coated finish and rubber balls. To learn more, dealers contact either: Lowrance/ Eagle Electronics at: 918-234-1710, www.lowrance.com for electronics mounts or Tite-Lok at: 800-848-3565, www.titelok.com for fishing rod holders. Consumers contact: Cabela's at: 800-237-4444 or www.cabelas.com. Contact the factory at 206-763-8361 or visit the R-A-M web site at: www.ram-mount.com.
Good fishing to you and remember to:Just R-A-M It!™

Bill Dance

Joe Thomas

Larry Nixon

TEAM R-A-M STAFF

"I can't imagine that everybody won't own one."

Pete Shepley
President, PSE

"... with the new camo outerwear, I can be confident that my outer clothing is not picking up stray scents and carrying them with me"

Jay Michael Strangis
Associate Editor
Petersen Outdoor
Group

"Just when I thought a great product couldn't get any better, Scent-Lok® offers yet another great surprise."

Dan Bertalan
Outdoor writer

"I'm going to wear my Scent-Lok® Camo over the liner for the ultimate in scent control. When it comes to scent, you can't be careful enough!"

Dr. David Samuel
Morgantown, West Virginia

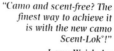

"Camo and scent-free? The finest way to achieve it is with the new camo Scent-Lok®!"

Larry Weishuhn
Wildlife Biologist/
Outdoor writer

"It's the ultimate in body camo and I wholeheartedly recommend it to serious hunters."

M.R. James
Editor/Founder
Bowhunter
Magazine

"... the best thing to happen to bow-hunting since the compound bow!"

Phil Phillips
Phil's Outdoor
Adventures

The new Scent-Lok® box!

"This phenomenal new product effectively diminishes two of the most powerful senses wild animals use... sight and smell. I personally would not hunt without my ScentLok® suit."

Dick Scorzafava
Outdoor writer, Lecturer

Scent-Lok® is now available in camo outerwear!

New Scent-Lok® Camo combines the scent elimination of activated charcoal with the concealment of camo in a convenient single-layer garment

- Available in Advantage,™ Mossy Oak® Break Up and Realtree® X-tra Brown
- Dramatically increases your chances of bagging a trophy buck!
- Reactivates by heating in your clothes dryer

Camo

ODOR ELIMINATING TECHNOLOGY

For more information,
call **1-800-315-5799**

Scent-Lok® Products are protected by
U.S. PATENT NO's. 5,383,236 and 5,539,930
Other patents pending.

Made in
the USA   ▲ **ALS ENTERPRISES**

821 W. Western Ave., Muskegon, MI 49441
616-725-6181 • Fax 616-725-7183

FAST
FASTER
FASTEST

The unique shape and the razor sharp grind of the **Chrome Alloy** stainless steel *LAZER* Blades and the new **Delta Wing Handle** system, make the *LAZER* family of hand and power ice augers the fastest and smoothest ever produced by **StrikeMaster**.

Hand

12-Volt

2.0 HP

3.0 HP

ICE TEAM

Sponsor

Field Tested

1997 Models

LAZER Hand Auger
4", 5", 6", 7", 8"

ELECTRA LAZER (12-V)
6", 7", 8"

LAZER Mag (2.0 H.P.)
6", 7", 8", 10"

XL-3000 (3.0 H.P.)
8", 10"

See your Local Dealer Today!

StrikeMaster®
Ice Augers

Big Lake   Minnesota

www.up-north.com/strikemaster

TR-1 *Liberator* for 4 Strokes Unveiled: NEW Remote Throttle & Autopilot!

Nautamatic's new *TR-1 Liberator* offers the ultimate and the only remote throttle control and autopilot steering system for four stroke outboards to 15hp. Throttle and steering are managed from anywhere on the boat with a single hand-held.

The new *TR-1 Remote Throttle* offers anglers precise speed control instantaneously with hundreds of distinct throttle positions unavailable manually. The Liberator's Autopilot compensates for wind and current to hold the trolling course through wind and waves.

Anglers can fish effectively, affordably and in a quiet, smoke-free environment with the new *TR-1 Liberator* on four stroke trolling motors.

The *TR-1 Liberator* is easy to use! Simply start the trolling motor, put it in gear, and point the boat in the direction you want to go. Set tiller throttle to idle, press FWD (or REV) on the deckmount to turn on *TR-1 Remote Throttle* and *TR-1 Autopilot*.

Pick up the remote and press the button forward to advance the throttle. Put out the gear, punch in the speed and sit back. The *TR-1 Liberator* will hold your speed and course through wind and waves!

Change course or speed (full throttle travel in less than two seconds) at will from anywhere, any position on the boat.

Press the idle/resume button on the remote to land fish, then again to return to original speed. Press kill button on the remote, and engine and autopilot shut down, electric throttle returns to idle and throttle electronics shut off.

The *TR-1 Liberator* sets you free to enjoy fishing, catching and your companions! Call Nautamatic toll free at 1-800-588-7655 for dealers and details on the *TR-1 Liberator*, your personal guide to better fishing and catching!

The Whole *Fishing* World Is In Your Hand with TR-1

Nautamatic Chauffeurs You! The _Only_ Autopilot, Remote Throttle for Outboard Trolling Motors

Remote Throttle available separately for four strokes. Autopilot for two and four stroke engines.

Autopilot runs your boat, throttle adjusts your speed! From Anywhere in the Boat

TR-1 'Sets You Free'
to fish more, catch more and have more boating fun!

1-800-588-7655
AUTOPILOT • NAUTAMATIC MARINE SYSTEMS, INC. • REMOTE THROTTLE

TRU-TURN® Hook More Fish!

Demonstrate Tru-Turn's Cam-Action to yourself! Discover why they are recommended for U.S. Military Survival Kits! And watch Gary Roach, Mark Martin and The Mr. Walleye Specialties Team **Hook More Fish** with Tru-Turn hooks.

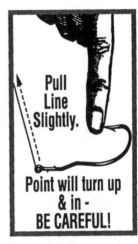

Pull Line Slightly.

Point will turn up & in - BE CAREFUL!

Daiichi® World's Sharpest Hooks

and we can prove it!

Here are some photographs of "brand name" hook points taken by an electron microscope. Things get ugly at 350 power – but Daiichi remains beautiful!

OFFICIAL HOOK
In-Fisherman
WALLEYE TRAIL

BRAND A

BRAND B

DAIICHI®

USED BY THE MR. WALLEYE SPECIALTY TEAM INCLUDING GARY ROACH, PERRY GOOD AND MARK MARTIN

THE SOFTEST RIDE ON THE WATER

THE ULTRARIDE™ SEAT SUSPENSION

Suspension system comprises tension springs in conjunction with oil hydraulic shock absorber.

- Absorbs more than 50% of shock and vibration keeping you fresh all day long.
- Affords better boat control and a sense of safety.
- Uses your boats factory seating.
- Maintenance Free.
- Will fit even the tallest rider.
- Fore and aft adjustments of up to 6 inches in 1/2 inch increments.
- Prevents uncomfortable bottoming out.
- Adjustable for rider weight from 110 to 265 pounds.
- Height is infinitely variable within 2-1/2 inches.

TOURNAMENT TESTED ON WALLEYE CIRCUITS.

Talbot Enterprises, Inc., 14045 Hwy 10, Elk River, MN 55330-1609

PHONE TOLL FREE 1-888-881-96663 FAX 612-241-8138
www.up-north.com/grammer

WAVE WACKERS®

"THE CHOICE OF THE PROS"

WAVE WACKERS are custom made to fit most boat and motor combinations. Trolling motor cutouts are optional. To order or for more information call WAVE WACKERS.

Custom Made Backtrolling Plates

Removable, virtually unbreakable, tinted Poly-carbonate shields with flexible Santoprene motor guards.

612/825-2323
Herrick Enterprises 4001 12th Ave. So. Mpls., MN 55407

ORDER BLANK

Yes! Please send me:

Name: _____

Address: _____

City: _____ **St.**_____ **Zip** _____

Number of Books @ $19.95: _____
(Year 'Round Walleyes)

Number of Videos @ $14.95: _____
(Night Walleye Fishing)

Shipping and handling: $3.00
$3.00 for 1 book or 1 video
(large orders would be more)

Michigan residents add 6% sales tax _____

            Total: _____

Make check or money order
payable to:

Mark Martin
P.O.B. 103
Twin Lake, MI 49457
Phone: 616-744-0330

THANK YOU!